Lee Kricher is the first person I know who transitioned a struggling and aging church into one that unchurched people love to attend. He's the expert I point people to with questions about transitioning a church. Now he's sharing the principles he learned. If you want to ensure that your church is positioned to reach the next generation, *For a New Generation* is a great place to start.

ANDY STANLEY, Senior Pastor, North Point Ministries

Rich in insight, difficult to put down, courage-inspiring, practical, and brutally honest, *For a New Generation* makes church revitalization seem invitingly doable—because it can be!

WARREN BIRD, Ph.D., Research Director, Leadership
Network; coauthor of twenty-eight books

Over 90 percent of American churches are either declining or growing more slowly than the community in which they are located. Here is the story of a church that went counter to the norm. Here is the story of a church that started reaching a new generation. Here is the story of a church where the seemingly impossible became possible in God's power. Read Lee Kricher's powerful story of Amplify Church for encouragement and insights. But above all, read it with the prayer that God will do a similar work in your church.

THOM S. RAINER, President and CEO of LifeWay Christian Resources;
author, *I Am a Church Member* and *Who Moved My Pulpit?*

I firmly believe that Jesus and his Church are the hope of the world. But what if a church no longer meets the needs of a younger generation and is at risk of irrelevance in its local community? I deeply admire Lee Kricher and his courageous leadership at Amplify Church to make the difficult but necessary changes to become the successful multigenerational church it is today—a place that seeks to shepherd its attendees toward an intimate relationship with Jesus Christ and lasting life transformation. *For a New Generation* tells a powerful leadership story that will resonate deeply with any pastor or church member who longs to be part of life-giving community of Jesus followers!

SANTIAGO "JIMMY" MELLADO, President and CEO of
Compassion International; coauthor, *Small Matters*

The challenge for most church leaders is that they listen to church planters talk at conferences, and then go home to a church that they need to *transition*. As someone who has both planted a church and transitioned a church, I can attest to the reality that they are not the same thing. Lee Kricher knows what he's talking about when it comes to church transition. You'll love his practical, inspiring approach and come to value him as a leader who really understands the dynamics in your church.

> **CAREY NIEUWHOF,** author, *Leading Change Without Losing It*;
> Founding Pastor, Connexus Church, Toronto

Becoming a true change maker requires not just the insight that change is needed but also a sound approach and the courage to take action. *For a New Generation* is an inspiring story of a church filled with courageous people committed to turning their church around. It's a unique guide that will help church leaders and members apply sound organizational change strategies to their own situations.

> **BRAD LOMENICK,** author, *H3 Leadership* and *The Catalyst Leader*

You will not be disappointed in this book! Lee Kricher is a seasoned church revitalizer and one who knows how to regrow a church. With the success of Amplify Church in Pittsburgh as his lab, Lee has developed a great book that will encourage you, challenge you, and lead your church to begin the effort of revitalization. The five practical strategies offered within these pages will help every church in need of revitalization. For the Church Revitalizer, this could be the most important book you purchase this year and there is none better to guide you than Lee Kricher.

> **TOM CHEYNEY,** Executive Director of Missions, Greater Orlando Baptist
> Association; Founder, Renovate National Church Revitalization
> Conference; author, *The Church Revitalizer as Change Agent*

I have known Lee Kricher for almost thirty years and have always respected his leadership excellence and pastor's heart. Within the last few years, I have watched as he stepped into an older church that had been in several years of decline, and he transitioned that organization not only into a rapidly growing church with multiple campuses but also into one of the leading churches in our city in reaching the next generation. As you read this book, you are reading Lee's observations—which are both sound and proven to work.

JEFF LEAKE, Lead Pastor, Allison Park Church (Assembly of God); Founder, *Reach Northeast* church planting network

Through real life application, Lee Kricher faces and addresses the challenges that not only the local church but many denominations are faced with today. He has embodied principles that are universal to every successful organization while balancing those with God's leading through the Holy Spirit, resulting in a ministry that is impacting the community. There's a takeaway for every leader who takes the time to read *For a New Generation*!

GERRY HINDY, President and CEO, AG Financial

Jesus said, "New wine must be put in fresh wineskins." *For A New Generation* answers the question, "How do you make an old wineskin fresh?" It contains principles and answers that many of us have been searching for. The journey of Amplify Church demonstrates that both the "old" and the "new" can be preserved. Every leader should be grateful for Lee Kricher's chronicling of this amazing journey.

BISHOP JOSEPH L. GARLINGTON, Sr., Presiding Bishop, Reconciliation! International Network of Churches and Ministries

If the church does not gain the heart and needed skill set to transition to the next generation, the consequences will be devastating. Lee Kricher has not written a book of theory, but a practical guide to getting it done. He has not only led a church back from the dead but has placed it into the hands of next generation leaders. Jesus prayed that our "fruit would remain". This book is an answer to this heart cry of our Savior.

JOHN NUZZO, Founding Pastor, Victory Family Church; Faculty, Rhema Bible Training College

We get the same impression when reading *For a New Generation* that we did when Lee Kricher spent a day with over a hundred church leaders from our conference. He has a humble approach that insists on the need for change without leaving people feeling judged or vilified. Lee does a masterful job of sharing the experiences, challenges, and delights that come with helping a church grow young. Don't be surprised if *For a New Generation* becomes a reference book that you return to repeatedly!

ALMA AND BRENT THOMPSON, Superintendents, Ohio
Conference of the Free Methodist Church

When I started my journey as a second career pastor seven years ago, I'd had decades of experience as a leader in the Air Force. I'd even taught leadership to senior officers at the Air War College. Yet I was unprepared for the challenge of leading transformation in a historic church. I'm grateful for Lee Kricher's unswerving commitment to bringing new life to churches like ours. *For a New Generation* is clear and focused and outlines an approach that pastors and lay leaders can work through together. I pray that it will lead many, many churches into God's better future.

TOM HALL, Senior Pastor, First Presbyterian Church of Pittsburgh

In writing out of his own experience, Lee Kricher has given us a tremendous gift in *For A New Generation*. Many churches want to grow but do not know how. Instead of seeking out new ways they continue to do what they've always done with greater sincerity. The results are still the same—continued decline. Lee writes from his experience of turning a declining congregation back to a place of effective growth by leading them to think and act differently. I know I will use this resource with churches under my supervision.

JOEL GARRETT, District Superintendent, the United Methodist Church

Lee Kricher's *For A New Generation* is a provocative read that challenges both pastors and congregational leaders to see that they can best honor their past by reshaping and developing ministries that will continue to reach the next generation. This is a significant book that calls the church as a whole to prayerfully create a vision of ministry that will clearly guide and direct its leaders as they faithfully consider which programs, ministries, and practices can best help the church to reach a new generation with the gospel of Jesus Christ.

WAYNE G. GILLESPIE, Pastor, Christ's Lutheran Church, Murrysville, PA

An urgent, hands-down, straight-up, no-nonsense game plan of how to grab the problem of church decline by the horns and, through the power of God and the collective wisdom of experienced pastors, flip it upside down. Lee Kricher has written a book that speaks across the boundaries of church traditions to all who have a desire to see the local church reach beyond itself and engage people with the gospel of Jesus Christ. This is not just a book for church leaders but for the passionate and the dispassionate whom they lead.

FR. JAMES MALLON, Pastor, Saint Benedict Parish, Halifax Nova Scotia; author, *Divine Renovation: Bringing Your Parish from Maintenance to Mission*

The key to future growth in the church is one that used to be taken for granted—effectively passing on our faith in Jesus Christ to the next generation. Lee Kricher beautifully combines his personal experience as a pastor with proven principles and strategies that would serve any congregation. This book is meant to be provocative, not prescriptive, and I would highly recommend it to any leader who is willing to stretch their thinking about their responsibility to future generations.

MATTHEW F. MANION, President & CEO, Catholic Leadership Institute

At Parish Catalyst, we bring together pastors and key members of their pastoral teams from across the country who are eager to grow their parishes in innovative ways. The principles found in *For a New Generation* have inspired these leaders to consider how to better reach the next generation-a critical factor in accelerating parish vitality and growth.

WILLIAM E. SIMON JR., Founder and Chairman, Parish Catalyst

What Lee Kricher has done with *For A New Generation* is provide a workable process for all those willing to take on the challenge of congregational revitalization. Written by someone who has lived the principles and the process personally, this is a valuable guide for pastors and parish leadership teams, regardless of their denomination. This book confirms that you can develop practical actions that can put your congregation on a road to vitality.

GREG PETRUCCI, Director of Evangelization, Roman Catholic Diocese of Greensburg

I am excited to imagine how Amplify Church's inspiring example of church revitalization can spur European church leaders to look to God to breathe new life into their struggling congregations and dying denominations. Lee Kricher wouldn't let his church die without a fight. This book can inspire new strategies for the battle that is just as real on this side of the Atlantic.

ANDY PECK, host, *The Leadership File*, Premier
Christian Communications, London UK

After thirty years of ministry, I went through a time of refocusing and reflection and prayerfully considered the possibility of planting a new church. With so many churches in Germany in decline, I needed to know: "What new approach should be taken?" I accepted an invitation from Lee Kricher to visit Amplify Church, a revitalized church in the northeast U.S. that was facing many of the same issues that we face. What I experienced inspired, guided, and encouraged me. The principles and strategies outlined in *For a New Generation* are a promising path to follow and helped us to successfully initiate a church for the next generation.

GOTTFRIED CLAUSSEN, Pastor, Christliches Zentrum, Amberg, Germany

Lee Kricher articulately and experientially lays out a road map for any church in any culture to be revitalized: to stop the decline and to breathe life back into a church. This book is not a collection of theories and ideas but sound principles that work in the real world! I hope that *For a New Generation* becomes a "best read" of pastors and leadership teams from the many churches in Australia and Asia that would greatly benefit from applying its strategies.

PETER PILT, International Director, Global Care Australia

Over a decade ago, Lee Kricher was an invaluable advisor to Chick-fil-A Inc. as we were developing the leadership competency model that still guides our leaders. Then and now, Lee consistently displays three qualities: humility, courage, and practicality. *For a New Generation* documents those same qualities being poured into the provocative and inspiring transformational journey of Amplify Church. A must read for all those interested in the Church and in the next generation!

MARK A. CONKLIN, Director, Staff Leadership Development, Chick-fil-A Inc.

For years, Lee Kricher was an Organizational Change Consultant and then Vice President of Leadership Development at DDI. He was a trusted advisor to our clients and an invaluable resource. It is no wonder that *For a New Generation* is such a powerful case study in applying proven change leadership principles in the local church. Lee is an excellent example of a catalyst leader—someone who knows that leadership is not lighting a fire under the team but igniting a fire within them.

TACY BYHAM, Ph.D., Chief Executive Officer, Development Dimensions International (DDI); coauthor, *Your First Leadership Job*

While this book focuses on the transformation of one church, its lessons resonate with any leader or organization struggling to change . . . or even survive. It is about the courage of one leader to let go of the past. It is a story about focusing on engaging a whole new generation, the building blocks of the future. Lee Kricher is leaving a legacy for decades to come.

DR. RICHARD WELLINS, Senior VP, Development Dimensions International; coauthor, *Your First Leadership Job*

Lee Kricher has created a masterful blueprint for driving change—simply elegant in teaching turnaround strategies embedded in a beautifully written success story that amplifies what can be done in two years.

PHIL HARKINS, Executive Chairman and Founder, Linkage, Inc

Lee Kricher's *For a New Generation* provides a blueprint to help churches grow in ways that are meaningful, purposeful, and relevant. The experience Lee gained during his years in corporate settings is applied here to a higher purpose. If your church needs to better reach the next generation, this book will map out the big picture, provide specific examples, and help to create momentum.

SUSAN BIXLER, author, speaker, and CEO, Bixler Consulting Group

For a New Generation does not provide another model to plug into your church but rather a guided path to examining every aspect of a local congregation, holding on to what is good and timeless and letting go of what is no longer working. It offers hope and encouragement to every church—dying and growing alike—as they embark on the journey to flourishing. It is an intrepid journey that will require courageous leadership. With this book in hand, you are not on that journey alone.

LISA PRATT SLAYTON, President, Pittsburgh Leadership Foundation

I have known Lee and Linda Kricher for almost four decades. They are articulate, bold, authentic, and creative leaders. It is not possible for every church to have Lee or Linda as a personal coach, but this book is the next best thing. *For a New Generation* contains proven principles and strategies that will equip any pastor or church member to more effectively attract and develop the kind of young and gifted leaders that are required for sustained church revitalization.

DR. JAY PASSAVANT, Founder/CEO, Passavant Leadership Group; author, *Seamless Succession: Simplifying Church Leadership Transitions*

FOR A NEW GENERATION

A PRACTICAL GUIDE FOR

REVITALIZING YOUR CHURCH

LEE KRICHER

ZONDERVAN

For a New Generation
Copyright © 2016 by Lee D. Kricher

This title is also available as a Zondervan ebook.
Visit www.zondervan.com/ebooks.

Requests for information should be addressed to:
Zondervan, 3900 *Sparks Dr. SE, Grand Rapids, Michigan 49546*

Library of Congress Cataloging-in-Publication Data

Names: Kricher, Lee, 1954- author.
Title: For a new generation : a practical guide for revitalizing your church / Lee
    Kricher.
Description: Grand Rapids : Zondervan, 2016.
Identifiers: LCCN 2016000206 | ISBN 9780310525226 (softcover)
Subjects: LCSH: Church renewal. | Intergenerational relations—Religious aspects—
    Christianity. | Church work with young adults.
Classification: LCC BV600.3 .K75 2016 | DDC 253—dc23 LC record available at
    http://lccn.loc.gov/2016000206

Cover design: *Tammy Johnson*
Cover photo: *Masterfile.com*
Interior design: *Kait Lamphere*

Printed in the United States of America

---

16 17 18 19 20 21 22 23 24 25 26 /DHV/ 15 14 3 12 11 10 9 8 7 6 5 4 3 2 1

To the members and attendees
of Amplify Church
whose devotion, prayers, and generosity
turned the dream of building a new generation church
into reality

CONTENTS

FOREWORD

Lee Kricher sat in my office in the spring of 2003 and told me he was considering returning to the role of senior pastor of the struggling and aging church he had helped start. I was pretty straightforward about how daunting it would be to initiate and implement the kind of significant change required for genuine church transformation. But he took on the challenge, and somehow he and the people of Amplify Church pulled it off. Their journey is documented in *For a New Generation*.

The focus of this book is on building a church that reaches—and will continue to reach—the next generation. While the specifics about what and how to change will vary from church to church, this book is a guide that contains universal principles of transformation. Any church leader or member, no matter the denomination, can benefit from reading it and working through the challenging questions posed in it.

It may seem too hard or too risky to change your church's ministry model to reach the next generation, especially if the people currently attending aren't bothered by the way things are. But changing your church's approach to ministry may not be the threat you think it is to your church's mission and existence. It may be the very thing that saves it.

Andy Stanley
Senior Pastor, North Point Ministries

INTRODUCTION

I grew up attending a Lutheran church with my mother. My wife, Linda, attended a Methodist church with hers. Both of our fathers were members of Catholic parishes. During my college years, I attended a Presbyterian church. I have served for many years as the pastor of a nondenominational church.

These churches have many things in common. They have remarkably similar statements of faith tied to the Apostles' Creed. They each have played a meaningful role in my life or the lives of people I love. And each one is at risk of being one of the thousands of churches that are closing their doors because they have lost touch with the next generation.

That statement may be painfully obvious if you belong to an aging church that is in decline. But even if you belong to a church with a healthy percentage of young adults and children, you cannot afford to underestimate the tendency of churches to get "older" over time and become less effective at connecting with the next generation.

Is it possible to ensure that a church reaches young adults and their children and continues to do so in the future? Is it possible to ensure that a church never has to live with the fear that its most vital days are in the past? I believe it is. I believe it is possible in the northeast United States where I live and where many young people have stopped regularly attending church. I believe it is possible in Europe where many young people have never regularly attended church. I believe it is possible in your church.

My definition of a new generation church is *a church with attendees whose average age is at least as young as the average age of the community in which the church exists.*

new generation church— a church with attendees whose average age is at least as young as the average age of the community in which the church exists

Any church can become a new generation church that reaches and continues to reach the next generation. I define the next generation simply as *those who are younger than the average age of the community in which your church exists.* This does not just include, of course, the children and grandchildren of your church members. It also includes the other children and young adults in your community, many of whom have no church background or experience. When we think of reaching the next generation and "our children," we must include them.

next generation— those who are younger than the average age of the community in which your church exists

The formation of a new generation church starts with an honest self-assessment. The average age in the United States is approximately thirty-seven years old. If the most recent census indicates that the average age of the community in which your church is located is thirty-seven years old and the average age of those attending your church is higher, you do not attend a new generation church. This should spark urgency, if not fear, in your heart.

The psalmist writes, "We will not hide these truths from

our children; we will tell the next generation about the glorious deeds of the LORD, about his power and his mighty wonders" (Psalm 78:4 NLT).

Of course, no Christian would purposely hide the timeless truths of Christianity from the next generation. But often we do, not because of the substance of our church—the timeless truths that we teach and believe—but because of our approach—the programs, ministries, and practices of our church. Our church's approach can be so unappealing to young adults and children that the message we are sending them is, "If you want to embrace the Christian faith, you will need to find another church. My church is designed primarily to be meaningful for me—not to reach you."

If our children reject the core truths of Christianity, may God have mercy on them. But if our children reject the core truths of Christianity because we have expected and assumed that they would accept our preferred approach to church, may God have mercy on us.

PERPETUAL CHURCH REVITALIZATION

Despite the large number of churches in decline today, far more is written about church planting than church revitalization. Church planting is a key part of the church's mission, and it is very close to God's heart. But how much progress are we making if, for every new church that is planted, another church is closing its doors? Forward thinking denominations like the Assemblies of God are proponents of doing both: vigorously planting new churches *and* revitalizing existing churches.[1]

Church planting is important but so is the revitalization of aging church congregations. Both are close to God's heart.

Church revitalization is often defined as *the process needed to turn a declining church into a growing church.* That definition makes sense but can just lead to a temporary season of improved church health because it does not emphasize reaching the next generation. I contend that we need to think in terms of *perpetual* church revitalization—*putting appropriate strategies in place to ensure that a church will connect with and stay connected with the next generation.*

perpetual church revitalization—putting appropriate strategies in place to ensure that a church will connect with and stay connected with the next generation

The apostle Paul's letters are written with the assumption that the local church would be filled with men and women of all ages. One pastor told me that he felt a need to attract older members because his church was filled with young adults in their twenties and thirties. He inherently knew that the church is healthier when every generation is well represented. Still, his experience is the exception. Most churches tend to become "aging" churches with fewer and fewer children and young adults attending church services. That is why none of us as church leaders or members should ever assume that our church will be able to avoid decline—and even extinction—unless we intentionally pursue perpetual church revitalization.

AMPLIFY CHURCH

Our church, Amplify Church, is a nondenominational church that was founded in the late 1970s in the eastern suburbs of Pittsburgh. As with most churches, it had experienced seasons of growth and seasons of decline. By 2003, however, the decline was so severe that the survival of the church was in serious doubt. Weekend attendance had fallen to under two hundred people. The church could not afford its monthly mortgage payments and had an arrangement with the bank to pay only the interest on the loan. The church building had been sorely neglected for years due to a lack of funds and was in dire need of major repairs. The most alarming issue, however, was that the average age of those attending the church was over fifty years old and grew older each year.

We decided to put our hearts into becoming a new generation church, to do whatever it would take to become *a church with attendees whose average age is at least as young as the average age of the community in which the church exists*. This was not an easy decision. The average age of the community served by our church was thirty-five years old. Our core beliefs did not need to change, but our approach to church had to change in many ways if we were going to lower the average age of our members and attendees by over fifteen years to match the average age of our community.

I would like to say that the journey over the following years went smoothly, but change seldom does. The *concept* of reaching young people was well received, but when things started to change in order to actually reach those young people, some people left the church and found a church that better matched their preferences. In fact, about a third of the people who had been attending our church left during the first two years after we started our change journey. One person who left noted, "I am supportive of the goal of reaching young people, but I didn't think we would need to change this much."

Fortunately, not everyone left. And new people started to attend Amplify Church. Within two years the average weekend attendance more than doubled to over four hundred people. Within five years, our average weekend attendance exceeded six hundred people. And within twelve years after embarking on our journey, the average attendance of the church grew to more than fourteen hundred people.

We had not become a megachurch. We were not even close to being the biggest church in our city. But we became healthy again, and we were growing for the first time in many years. The majority of our new attendees had not been attending church anywhere. And perhaps most significantly, every generation was once again well represented in our church. The average age of those attending was just under thirty-five years old, the average age of our community. We had transformed into a new generation church.

ABOUT THIS BOOK

This book highlights choices and changes we made at Amplify Church with the goal of reversing our decline and getting reconnected to the next generation. Each chapter highlights one of five practical strategies that made a positive difference for us:

Strategy #1: Adopt a New Mindset
Strategy #2: Identify the Essentials
Strategy #3: Reduce the Distractions
Strategy #4: Elevate Your Standards
Strategy #5: Build a Mentoring Culture

We employed these five strategies roughly in chronological order, but there was definitely overlap. In fact, we started to take some action on all five strategies within the first three months of our change journey. This book details the actions we took.

Your church is unique. You cannot and should not copy the actions that another church has taken. I share the specific actions we took to be *provocative*—not *prescriptive*. While you may not resonate with the specific actions we took at Amplify Church, those actions will give you a sense of what it looks like when a congregation implements these five strategies.

Over the years, as I have talked with and observed other leaders, I have come to believe that the five strategies that led to our changes are sound. Prayerful discussion among the leaders of your church and conversations with your congregation will help you to determine how to apply these strategies in your church.

Please note that this book is not about changing your church's statement of faith or core beliefs to make them more attractive to next-generation thinking. Instead, it is about evaluating and changing, as needed, your church's programs, ministries, and practices. It is about adopting and applying principles that are inspired by a deep-seated commitment that we cannot allow the faith that we value so highly to be lost to our children without a fight.

Although this book is built around practical strategies that sparked specific actions, prayer was definitely one of the major factors in the turnaround of our church. Tom Cheyney, founder of the Renovate National Church Revitalization Conference, writes, "People ask me all the time what is the key ingredient to church revitalization. Most want a magic pill that will fix their dying church with little or no effort. But without a doubt the single most important ingredient to renewal is the power that comes from intercessory prayer."[2]

Many great books on prayer are available, and while it will not be the focus of this book, if you do everything suggested in this book and fail to pray, your church will not succeed in reaching the next generation. All lasting change and revitalization begins as we acknowledge our dependence on God and ask him to do what only he can do.

WHO THIS BOOK IS FOR

Because my hope is that this book provokes change, I have written it for both church leaders and church members. Church leaders and members must work together to ensure that a church does not slowly fade.

If you are a pastor, you will likely find that there are times when this book gets "in your face" and says things you don't want to hear. I cannot imagine a church embarking on a journey of genuine revitalization without the leadership of their pastor. You are a leader because you are called to lead. And though you may not be able to implement significant change on your own, you can inspire and rally others to embrace change.

If you are a church member or church staff member and you have been given this book to read, consider it a compliment. You are obviously seen as a person who has the ability to influence others. Read it prayerfully and resist the natural tendency to be defensive and fight for the status quo. You are in a unique position. You can be a blocker of change or a catalyst for change. If you choose to be a catalyst for change, you can help to pave the way for a bright future for your church.

Finally, if you are a seminary student or a seasoned pastor who is prayerfully considering what God's will is for your future ministry, don't rule out the possibility that he may want you to lead a declining church into revitalization. Many will advise you that it is easier to plant a new church. They are probably correct. But God's will is seldom based on the easiest path. Helping to turn around a fading church can be immensely rewarding, and this book will give you tools to do it.

SUGGESTED APPROACH

Consider approaching this book from the very beginning as a framework for action. In other words, don't just read the book for information. As you read, ask God to help you to have a genuine openness of mind and heart. At Amplify Church we tried to avoid placing limitations on who God could use to inspire us. We studied what other churches were doing to reach the next generation. We tried to avoid dismissing new ideas with statements like, "That would never work for us."

I recall some of the initial responses the people of our declining church had when we heard about churches that were growing and thriving.

- "Of course those churches are growing; they are in the middle of the Bible Belt. Pastors there just have to roll out of bed and a thousand people show up."
- "It's easy for that church to grow. They are located in the fastest-growing part of our city. We are located in an area where there is practically zero growth."
- "Those growing churches don't have the same dynamics and issues that we have. No church could have the same dynamics and issues that we have."

Every one of those responses held some truth, but each one could have easily become an excuse for not trying. As you are reading this book, don't accumulate excuses; pray for God to develop your spiritual imagination, to give you a vision for what he can do as you trust him in faith.

Perhaps the most common objection to change that I hear from church leaders is, "We could never do that because of the type of church we are." Obviously, I don't know what type of church you belong to. Your church may be nondenominational, like ours, or you may belong to a historic denomination with an established structure and lines of authority. While you will definitely need to process what you read in light of your specific context, your context should not be used as an excuse to avoid taking action.

I recently read an inspiring book about church revitalization called *Rebuilt: Awakening the Faithful, Reaching the Lost, and Making Church Matter.*[3] It is about the change journey of a Roman Catholic parish near Baltimore, Maryland. The leaders and people of this parish embraced principles strikingly similar to those contained in this book, and they went from being a dying parish to one of the healthiest parishes in the country. Does your denomination or association of churches give you less local autonomy than the Roman Catholic Church?

In talking with church leaders from a variety of denominational backgrounds and church structures, I have found that many are living inside an imaginary fence. You probably have more leeway than you think to make changes in your church. In many cases, you may even be able to get support from your denomination. As denominational leaders consider the growing number of declining churches under their oversight, many are focusing their time and energy on encouraging churches to explore new approaches rather than enforcing denominational constraints. If you are a denominational leader reading this, I hope this is true of you. Even if doing so pushes you out of your comfort zone, you can choose to leverage your influence by openly encouraging churches to plan and implement appropriate changes that could help them to regain health and vitality.

You probably have more leeway than you think to make changes in your church.

THE PACE OF CHANGE

During several years when I was not in full-time ministry, I served as an executive coach for corporate leaders. Many of these leaders were involved in helping their organizations navigate major organizational change. I observed that rapid, sweeping change was more effective than slow, incremental change. Sometimes leaders move slowly, thinking they are being kind or respectful to those living through the changes. But more often than not, slow, incremental change turns out to be torturous for all involved.

More often than not, slow, incremental change turns out to be torturous for all involved.

The dynamics of church leadership differ from that of corporate leadership, but some leadership principles are based on human nature and the way people respond to change. If we look to church history, perhaps the biggest change in the early church was the decision to invite non-Jews to become Christians. What would have happened if a slow, incremental approach to change had been adopted? Likely, a plan would have been put in place to give church members a few decades to get used to the idea. Such a long-range plan would have had disastrous effects on the growing identity of the Christian church. Instead, Peter and Paul and the council of leaders made decisions that led to rapid, sweeping change.

Given the urgency of our mission, I am not a fan of slow, incremental change because it puts the church's mission on hold. My conviction is that with appropriate planning and courage, most of the changes your church needs to make to better connect with the next generation can be made within a two-year time frame. This is roughly the time it took us to make most of the significant changes at Amplify Church. And while some churches may move more quickly and others will take a bit longer, this book is written with a two-year time frame for change in mind.

IT IS WORTH THE FIGHT

You won't be dishonoring your church's past if you consider changing the way you will do things in the future. You honor the past by remembering and celebrating the many ways God has used your church. But you also honor the past by planning for the future so that your church continues to have a positive impact on future generations. Churches that close their doors no longer honor the past. Only those churches that survive and thrive will have a story to tell to their children.

Reading and discussing with others the strategies for change in this book will lead to conflict—both internal and external. You will be torn between fighting to maintain your current approach to church and fighting for an approach to church that will better reach the next generation. No amount of logic will enable you to escape this conflict. But if you work through the conflict, you can help to create a church that will thrive for generations to come. It is worth the fight. Are you ready?

CHAPTER 1

WAITING FOR THINGS TO COME BACK AROUND

Pittsburgh, Pennsylvania, is known as the Steel City. Pittsburgh was America's leading steel manufacturer for over a century, providing steel that helped to build the nation from the Empire State Building to the Golden Gate Bridge. Unpredictably, because of the changing world economy, most of the steel mills in Pittsburgh were shut down by the late 1980s. Pittsburgh has since experienced a remarkable transformation and has become a world leader in technology, education, and health care, but the years at the end of the steel era were traumatic ones.

I recall a conversation I had during that time with a steelworker in his midthirties. He had been laid off by Homestead Steel Works, one of the many steel mills that had ceased operations. The mill where he had worked was to be torn down to make way for a water park and a shopping plaza. When I asked him what he planned to do for a living, he replied, "I am not changing careers. My grandfather was a steelworker, my father was a steelworker, and I am a steelworker. I'm waiting for things to come back around."

> No matter how hard we might wish, some things will never ... go back to the way they were.

That never happened. The changes in the steel industry were not temporary. Unfortunately, no matter how hard we might wish, some things will never come back around. Some things will never go back to the way they were.

REALITIES THAT CANNOT BE IGNORED

When I was growing up in the eastern suburbs of Philadelphia, I attended church every weekend. There was never a question of whether or not we would go. It was expected. It was the right thing to do—a social obligation, of sorts. Most of my friends felt the same way. Yet now, just one generation later, very few young adults feel any sense of obligation to attend church. Some have never attended a church before. Others don't even think about it. It's not even on their radar. The change in cultural expectations is so dramatic that it is hard for many of us to process.

Most of us don't need statistics to be convinced that things have changed, but research can help us see why we need to take action. Findings by the Barna Group reported in the book *Churchless* confirm that the United States has seen a significant decline in church attendance: "The number of unchurched adults in the United States has increased by more than 30 percent in the past decade. As of 2014, the estimated number of unchurched adults stood at 114 million. Add to that the roughly 42 million children and teenagers who are unchurched and you have 156 million US residents who are not engaged with a Christian church."[1]

Even more disconcerting is the Barna Group's finding that

the younger a person is, the less likely he or she is to attend church services.[2] Pew Research Center's 2014 Religious Landscape Study confirms this trend, finding that one-third of Americans under age thirty have no religious affiliation.[3] I have talked with church leaders and members who acknowledge these trends and lament with one another about the absence of young people at church. Some express nostalgia about the past and hope and pray that young people will start attending church again. They are waiting for things to come back around.

After spending several decades studying local churches that had ceased to exist, Thom S. Rainer in *Autopsy of a Deceased Church* wrote, "The most pervasive and common thread of our autopsies was that the deceased churches lived for a long time with the past as hero. They held on more tightly with each progressive year. They often clung to things of the past with desperation and fear. And when any internal or external force tried to change the past, they responded with anger and resolution: 'We will die before we change.' And they did."[4]

Obviously, some young adults prefer to attend churches that are similar in approach to the churches their parents or grandparents attended. And many churches that have instituted little change to their approach are healthy and growing. Thus, a leader or member of a church in decline may be tempted to hope that young people will suddenly start returning to their church without any changes having to be made. That would be unwise.

Each church must wrestle with its own realities. As a church leader or member, you must pay close attention to the message the children and young adults of your church and community are sending to you. They will not picket out in front of the church or send letters to the church board, but they will send a clear message. The way the next generation tells you that your church has lost touch with them is simple—they stop coming.

The way the next generation tells you that your church has lost touch with them is simple—they stop coming.

Rainer proposes a course of action for leaders of dying churches, churches that are not making the kinds of changes they need to make to survive. In what he refers to as "death with dignity," Rainer challenges these leaders to consider options such as selling the church property and giving the funds to another church. "What can you do in the last days of your congregation to make sure that your church's death can actually make a difference for the good for the Kingdom?"[5]

If it is too late for your church to turn things around, perhaps you would be wise to plan for such death with dignity. In some cases that may be the only option available. But for most churches, an alternative is available. Instead of surrendering to the idea that your church will cease to exist as a significant influence in your community, you can take action. You can come to grips with the fact that the world is changing and that you cannot approach church the same way as you did in the past and expect to see a sudden influx of children and young adults. You can decide to make the changes necessary to build a church that will effectively reach and continue to reach the next generation.

AN UNEXPECTED INVITATION

In early 2003 I was contacted by a member of the board of directors of what is now called Amplify Church. At the time, my wife, Linda, and I were living in Atlanta, and I was regional vice president for an international leadership development and executive coaching firm. We loved Atlanta, both the climate and our friends. The board member called me because I was the founding pastor of the church and had served as pastor during the late 1970s and 1980s. He knew that my wife and I were concerned about the health of the church and its future. Still, as he described the steep decline of the church and asked if I would consider becoming a candidate for the open senior pastor position, my answer was easy—I said no.

But the church didn't give up that easily. Over the next several months the phone calls kept coming. I was encouraged multiple times to pray about taking the position, something I did not want to do. I had not been in full-time ministry for more than a decade, and I had little interest in returning at that time. I was fifty years old, and the next ten years promised to be the best earning years of my career. A two-thirds cut in pay to go back into ministry as the pastor of a dying church had little appeal.

Financial considerations aside, the bigger problem was that I had no confidence that I had what it took to turn the church around. I had a difficult time as it was trying to get my two teenage daughters to attend church with us! For years, every Sunday morning our home turned into a battlefield as both of our daughters refused to get in the car to go to church because they believed it was boring and irrelevant. Every Sunday morning, I acted like a crazy man and threatened them loudly enough for the neighbors to hear until they finally got into the car. Each week we arrived at church late and left early. I had just enough time at church to ask for forgiveness for how I had acted that morning. Given my experience with my own family, I had little confidence that I could motivate anyone to go to church.

One thing did intrigue me enough, though, to at least consider the request from Pittsburgh. A little more than a year earlier, we had been invited to attend North Point Community Church. I had heard it was a contemporary church, so I assumed that it was not very spiritual, but we accepted the invitation and attended a service. One of our daughters was off at college, but I convinced our other daughter to join us.

The experience was very different from what I had expected. The music was youthful and upbeat, but all generations were well represented among the congregation. The message by the pastor, Andy Stanley, was not only engaging—it had a depth that I did not expect. It challenged me in a way I had not been challenged in years. But I almost went into shock after the service ended. My daughter was walking beside me and made a call to her best friend on her cell phone before we even exited the building. I heard her say, "You are coming to church with me next week."

My experience at North Point Community Church opened my mind and heart to the idea of serving as a pastor again. As we attended North Point, I witnessed lives that were genuinely changed, including mine. I began inviting work colleagues and friends to attend church with us. I knew that people of all ages would find the church to be engaging and relevant to their lives. One thing was clearly evident: the people of North Point Community Church had a mindset that they would do whatever it would take to reach the next generation.

"IT'S TIME TO KICK BACK"

After much prayer and consideration, I let the board of directors of Amplify Church know that I would candidate for the open position of senior pastor. My experience at North Point had cracked open the door of possibilities. I also had a lingering sense of obligation that I could not just watch the church I had helped to start go down the tubes.

According to the church by-laws, a congregational vote was needed to choose the person who would fill the open position of pastor. I was advised that it would be wise for me to hide my intentions to lead the church into a season of major change until after the congregational vote. But I felt that this would be deceptive. Instead, I chose to be crystal clear up front about the need for radical, strategic change. I spoke about this in the messages I shared prior to the congregational vote. I made it clear that those who did not want significant change should vote no.

I also tried to be candid about why it was so important for the church to reconnect with the next generation. I cast a vision of a church that was no longer in a state of decline, that would once again be filled with people from every generation, and that would once again make a difference in our city. I ended my message before the congregational vote with these words: "The devil has kicked this church around long enough. It's time to kick back."

I would have been at peace if there were not enough votes for me to be called as the new pastor. We would have continued with our life in Atlanta, and I would have slept peacefully knowing that I had responded to God's promptings and had at least thrown my hat into the ring. The result was that more than 90 percent of those voting voted yes. When all was said and done, I was installed as pastor of Amplify Church in September 2003.

STRATEGY #1: ADOPT A NEW MINDSET

I knew that we had a lot of work to do. First of all, I sensed that any plan for effective change in our church had to start with the congregation adopting a new mindset. In his letter to the church of Rome, Paul encouraged the Romans to "be transformed by the renewing of your mind" (Romans 12:2). Personal transformation always begins with a change in mindset. The same is true of organizational transformation. In fact, the other four strategies for building a new generation church all hinge on this first strategy.

The most important change of mindset needed at Amplify Church was apparent. We had been building our church around this unspoken assumption: "If it was good enough for me, it is good enough for our children." Now we had to stop assuming. We had to turn that statement into a question. We needed to start building our church around one key question: "What will it take to reach our children?"

This was a formidable challenge for the people of our church. Though they had voted me in as their new pastor, most of the people who were currently attending the church were there because they were okay with how things were. For the most part, they felt that young people should come to the church as it was, no changes needed. Discussions about the lack of young people in our church usually focused on what was wrong with the next generation rather than on how we needed to change as a church. People were waiting, hoping and praying that things would come back around. I knew we would never change unless we adopted a new mindset.

> **We needed to start building our church around one key question: What will it take to reach our children?**

THE FASTEST DYING CHURCH IN THE CITY

I took on the role of pastor knowing that we had many challenges to face. Our rapidly declining attendance and giving were big problems. Unfortunate but not shocking was the fact that almost all of those who voted no for me to become pastor immediately left the church. It didn't help matters that several people who left were proclaiming that the changes I was proposing would "kick the Holy Spirit out of the church." I remember thinking at the time that if the Holy Spirit had been leading this church, he had been doing a really bad job. But I didn't say that. Still, I couldn't help but feel defensive at the criticism.

Our church building was in terrible shape. We had fewer

than two hundred people supporting a fifty-thousand-square-foot facility on twenty acres of land. Many things had to be replaced. Several heating and air-conditioning units were not functioning. Replacing just one of them would cost us more than a month of offerings. The entire roof had to be replaced as well. A recent rainstorm had filled the grand piano with water through one of the many leaks. The parking lots were gravel and mud. In the middle of one of the parking lots was a block building with no roof and half-finished concrete block walls. Construction had started ten years earlier on this "community center," but it had been abandoned due to lack of funds. The building permit had expired, and one of the church members had a personal garden growing inside.

As bad as the building issues were, I was even more discouraged by the reputation our church had in the community as a troubled church with big problems. Although Amplify Church had a rich history and had positively influenced the lives of many people, it was obvious to anyone who cared that the church was a shell of what it once had been. The handful of members who remained would occasionally be asked by their friends and neighbors, "Why would you still go to *that* church?"

Despite the problems with the building and our reputation in the community, the biggest problem by far, in my estimation, was that the average age of the church attendees was about the same age that I was at the time—fifty years old. The most recent census data indicated that the average age of those living in the area around us in the eastern suburbs of Pittsburgh was thirty-five years old. Amplify Church was not even close to being a new generation church—*a church with attendees whose average age is at least as young as the average age of the community in which the church exists.* We had a handful of young families and a few children attending, but we had to be honest: we were one of the fastest dying churches in the city.

THE GUIDING COALITION

I knew that I had the responsibility as the pastor to take the lead in our church revitalization efforts, starting with the adoption of a new mindset. I also knew that I would not be able to lead significant change on my own. I could manage the communication and oversee the overall implementation of change, but it would be crucial to have the right people on board to make it successful. In his classic book about organizational transformation called *Leading Change*, John Kotter writes,

> No one individual, even a monarch-like CEO, is ever able to develop the right vision, communicate it to large numbers of people, eliminate all the key obstacles, generate short-term wins, lead and manage dozens of change projects, and anchor new approaches deep in the organization's culture. Weak committees are even worse. A strong guiding coalition is always needed—one with the right composition, level of trust, and shared objective.[6]

Kotter speaks of a "guiding coalition," the group of people whose support and involvement are most crucial in making significant change happen. In a church, this would include key staff leaders and key lay leaders, with the coalition led by the senior pastor. Kotter recommends that the members of the guiding coalition have one or more of four characteristics—*position power, expertise, credibility,* and *leadership.* He considers it equally important to avoid people whose egos or trust-killing behavior would undermine any possible progress.

guiding coalition—the group of people whose support and involvement are most crucial in making significant change happen

Amplify Church operated as a congregational church with the board of elders and board of directors and the committees they had established making decisions regarding the direction of the church. So our guiding coalition, for the most part, consisted of the combined board of elders and board of directors and me. Two members of the board of elders who were in open opposition to my leadership left the church when I was voted in as pastor. I asked another member of the board of elders who was clearly aligned with those who had left the church to leave his position. You will need wisdom and courage to avoid adding the wrong people to your guiding coalition, but making these difficult decisions early on in the process is crucial. You will have enough battles to fight without having open adversaries on the team you put together to lead the change.

Depending on your situation, it may be wise or even necessary to identify an external coach who can help the members of the guiding coalition to reach a prayerful consensus on the nature and timing of changes the church should make to better reach the next generation. This coach could also serve as a sounding board for the pastor during the most crucial months of decision making and change implementation. Don't be afraid to invest in hiring such a person who can bring much-needed perspective and insight. For instance, a pastor who is a close friend of mine hired an external consultant to help the leadership team of his church navigate through a time of major organizational change. He indicated that the objective guidance and facilitation of the consultant helped to bring quicker resolution to the disagreements that naturally arose among members of the leadership team. Each situation is unique, but an external consultant can help the change process to go more quickly and smoothly.

THE CHANGING MINDSET AT AMPLIFY CHURCH

In the first three months after I was voted in as pastor, we did a few things to begin planting seeds for a new mindset. Because my experience at North Point Community Church had led to a revolution in my own thinking, I took the members of our guiding coalition (which we simply called our leadership team) and their spouses on a "field trip" to experience North Point. I wanted them to see in person the impact that a new generation church could have in a community. We attended weekend services and toured the children's and youth areas, and then we met together to discuss what we had experienced. It proved to be a transformational experience. They had lived so long inside the walls of our dying church that they had lost touch with what a healthy church with all generations well represented was like. A significant change in mindset of those in the guiding coalition took place in that single weekend.

Every person returned to Pittsburgh asking, "What will it take to reach our children?"

With this in mind, I would encourage you to find some concrete, real-life examples of churches that are reaching the next generation. Getting outside of your own building and experiencing God's work in another church can inspire new ideas and break old mindsets in ways that discussions and debates never will. Consider a field trip (or "vision trip") to other churches with your key leaders as a way of jump-starting the discussion.

Members of our leadership team also read books and articles about church revitalization and reaching the next generation. Their reading and our subsequent discussions had a big impact on how they viewed things at our church. In addition to the reading, we studied the characteristics of courageous change leaders throughout history, such as Ernest Shackleton, the Arctic explorer who led his crew on a miraculous journey of survival, and Joshua Chamberlain, the Union officer whose leadership helped to shape the outcome of the Battle of Gettysburg and ultimately the Civil War. Naturally, the members of our leadership team began to share what they were learning with other church members. Their enthusiasm for change and their openness to thinking in new ways began to spread to the rest of the church.

From the moment I was voted in as pastor, I spoke regularly during weekend services about God's heart for the next generation and our responsibility to build a bridge. I challenged church members to start thinking in terms of doing whatever it would take to reach the young people of our community.

I considered every message to be a critical opportunity to help our church adopt a new mindset. I did not use that time to criticize the past or to criticize those who disagreed with change. Instead, I cast a positive vision about what the future could hold. The weekend messages were the single most powerful vehicle for changing the mindset of our church.

> **The weekend messages were the single most powerful vehicle for changing the mindset of our church.**

Within the first few months after I assumed the role of pastor, we initiated small group Bible studies and encouraged every member to attend. Our first study was Rick Warren's *The Purpose Driven Life*. The majority of those attending the church joined a small group through this initiative. The readings and our discussions revolved around our God-given purpose as Christians to make a difference in our community and world. This was a significant turning point because people were not just hearing a message on the weekend about reaching the next generation. They were also discussing in their small groups our God-given purpose as individuals and as a church to make a difference in our community and world.

Finally, one of the most important things that helped to shift our thinking as a church was personal conversation. As the mindset of those on the guiding coalition began to change, we all went out of our way to speak face-to-face with as many church members as possible in one-on-one settings. Our goal was to spark passion for building a new generation church. Along with everything else we were doing, these conversations were critical in the adoption of a new mindset throughout the church. While it is good to focus on group plans and communicating through preaching, don't neglect the power of personal conversations. They are key to spreading the vision and calling people to personally get involved.

THE ROLE OF THE PASTOR

One key to implementing a strategy for change and the adoption of a new mindset is understanding and embracing the role the pastor plays. Unless the pastor steps into the role of change leader, a church will not experience significant change. Some pastors are more comfortable providing care in a shepherding role than leading organizational change, but people need their pastor to lead them into the future. Lay leaders in declining churches without a pastor need to recruit a pastor with a passion to build a new generation church and let that person lead the way.

Unless the pastor steps into the role of change leader, a church will not experience significant change.

If you are a pastor, your church and community need you to become a better leader so that you can lead the way. In their book *Your First Leadership Job*, Tacy Byham and Rich Wellins of Development Dimensions International use the word *catalyst* when defining effective leadership.

> Much like an ingredient that induces a chemical reaction, a catalyst leader is someone who ignites action in others. . . . The common characteristic in great catalysts is their passion to become better leaders. They're

constantly building their leadership skills. They're also introspective—looking in the mirror every day and asking what they could do to become better leaders.[7]

If you are a pastor, do not shy away from leading change even if you feel, *That is just not who I am.* Your love for the people and your passion for the future of your church will provide the necessary motivation for you to step out of your comfort zone and become a catalyst leader. Asking and trusting God for the wisdom, favor, and courage you need is not presumptuous.

Consider this: if the role of change leader is delegated to someone other than the pastor, the congregation will naturally wonder about the pastor's commitment to change. Moreover, whoever is appointed to lead the change may steer the process in unwanted directions, especially if that person is highly opinionated and has gained credibility because of the pastor's deference to him or her. I have seen such scenarios undermine the pastor, derail the change process, and even split the church. If you are the pastor of a church in need of revitalization, you must step up.

Of course *all* of the paid staff must be fully committed to making the necessary changes. You will need all hands on deck for the hard work of change, and the church cannot afford to have any person who is lukewarm about reaching the next generation hold a precious spot on staff. Such a person might even end up affirming members who oppose the needed changes! Hopefully, any paid staff member whose heart is not in the change process will realize that it is best for all concerned to find a church in which to serve that better fits his or her convictions. If such staff members do not come to this realization on their own, graciously let them go as soon as you possibly can. Every penny you save on the salary of a staff member who is not fully on board can be used to help create a new generation church.

LEADERSHIP STYLE

In general, I am a big believer in high-involvement leadership. High-involvement leadership is about directly involving those you are leading in making decisions about the organization's future. Since involvement builds commitment, the more you can involve people in deciding what changes will be made or how the changes will be implemented, the more they will be committed to making the changes work. That said, a high-involvement leadership style is not the right approach in *every* situation. Aaron's high-involvement leadership approach with the people of Israel while Moses was on Mount Sinai was disastrously foolish.

A high-involvement leadership style is not the right approach in *every* situation.

One of the change projects I led when I worked as an executive coach was with a group of chemical plants located in various parts of the country. Senior management wanted the changes in every plant to be made and implemented using a high-involvement approach. This worked well in every plant—except one.

In one of the plants located in the Midwest, a team of managers, operators, and maintenance workers met together over several months to analyze the reasons why the plant was not profitable. Together they agreed that the biggest problem was that maintenance workers were not on site twenty-four hours a day to keep the manufacturing process going without interruption. However, the maintenance workers at the plant had seniority, and they preferred to work only the daylight shift. They also enjoyed receiving up to twice their hourly wage when they were called in to help during the evening and early morning shifts.

After several months of analyzing the situation, the maintenance worker with the most seniority presented the consensus recommendation: "We will just try to make things work better as they are. We recommend no changes." All the workers at the plant lost their jobs less than two years later when the plant had to be closed.

Each leader and pastor needs to adopt a style of leadership that best matches their situation. In the first two years after accepting the call to pastor Amplify Church, I adopted a more "leader-driven" approach to change as opposed to a high-involvement approach. I actively championed the five key strategies and related actions that I was convinced were necessary to turn things around. I did not passively stand by hoping that people would naturally come to consensus about these changes. I led.

I knew that, in time, I would adopt a more high-involvement leadership approach for the long-term health of the church. Pastors (and corporate executives) who maintain a strong and ongoing leader-driven approach eventually wear out the people who look to them for leadership. But as the pastor–change leader, don't be afraid to take a leader-driven approach for a season if that is what it will take for your church to become healthy again. Sometimes a stronger hand is needed to break old habits and instill new values.

Decades ago I was told by a seasoned pastor, "Someone is going to lead your church. If you abdicate that role, there will always be someone who is happy to take your place." When you look at Moses, Joshua, Deborah, Nehemiah, Peter, Paul, and other leaders who are profiled in the Scriptures, you don't see people who led with timidity. Though they initially may have been hesitant to take on the role of leader, they ended up leading with God-inspired boldness. Bold changes seldom occur without bold leadership. As the pastor, you are the change leader, and you need to be willing to embrace whatever leadership style is necessary to lead your church to become the church God intends for it to be.

FOR CHURCH MEMBERS

If you are a committed church member, you already know that your pastor cannot bring revitalization to your church without a lot of help. You can play a vital role in the revitalization of your church. You can decide to become a change agent who does everything possible to help make the change work instead of being a blocker of change. This may even mean deciding to support changes you may not agree with.

Becoming a change agent requires a willingness to let go of your preferences regarding the church programs, ministries, and practices that need to change to better reach the next generation. Remember, the core beliefs and values of your church are not changing. Paul encouraged the Ephesians to humbly "make every effort to keep the unity of the Spirit through the bond of peace" (Ephesians 4:3). Those words may seem to be impossible to live when you are trying to agree about significant changes in your church! Know that your prayers, your attitude, and your words will have more impact than you might imagine.

Unfortunately, some church members try to take control in order to keep things the way they are. One pastor shared with me how a church member came to him and said, "This is my church, not yours. I was here before you came, and I will be here long after you leave." Don't be surprised to hear something similar from people in your church, especially those who have been around a long time.

In their book *Replant: How a Dying Church Can Grow Again*, Darrin Patrick and Mark DeVine write about a common predicament that paralyzes churches from becoming what God intends for them to be. "Well-meaning members lose sight of their role as servants and become increasingly focused on controlling the very church they are called to serve. When a serving heart is replaced by a controlling heart, division is bound to ensue."[8]

If you are a church member and you are in opposition to the changes your pastor is proposing to more effectively reach the next generation, your best contribution to the church may be to leave in order to find a church that fits your preferences and is not interested in changing. I was shocked and saddened when a long-standing member of our church stated that she didn't care what happened after she died as long as the church stayed the way it was until the day her funeral was held. I was sad that she left the church and that her funeral was conducted elsewhere. Still, I was glad that the church did not put its mission on hold to wait for her to depart for heaven. The church is bigger than the wants, needs, and preferences of any single individual. The church exists for God's sake, and it must be committed to God's mission of reaching people. God's priorities and purposes for the church need to be front and center.

If, as a committed church member, you decide to stay in your church during its revitalization, don't be a person who opposes change or adopts a neutral "wait and see" attitude. A more noble decision would be to adopt a new mindset. Step out in faith. Pray for the process. Trust that God is at work. Don't give in to fears or put your own preferences before the larger mission of reaching the next generation. Get behind your pastor with your prayers and support, and give your church a fighting chance. This can be an extremely rewarding role as you see your church turn around and begin to reach people in your community, including the next generation, more effectively.

WE WERE ON OUR WAY

I sincerely wish that everyone at Amplify Church had adopted our new mindset of doing whatever it would take to reach the next generation. This would have made the change process much less challenging for everyone involved. Not surprisingly, we had some people who just could not or would not get behind the goal of building a new generation church.

I remember the day when one of our members pulled me

aside. He also happened to be one of our biggest givers. He said to me, "The kind of changes that are being discussed are going to cost a lot of money, and the kids you are trying to reach don't have checkbooks." He was stating two indisputable facts. Then, to my dismay, he added, "If you go through with these changes, I'm leaving the church, and my checkbook is going with me." That was not easy to hear. The reality is that if too many people had responded that way, our story would have turned out very differently.

Fortunately, most people did not respond in this manner. Most people caught on to the vision. They embraced the hope that we, as a church, could reconnect with the next generation. Most people took the leap of faith that our church could become healthy again with all generations well represented. In fact, the definitive change in mindset that we needed as a church did not take several years to kick in. Of the five strategies that shaped our change process, adopting a new mindset was by far the quickest and easiest. We saw a tangible shift within a few months.

We still had very few young adults or children attending our church, but most members were now openly embracing new ideas. They talked about the importance of rebuilding our church around the question "What will it take to reach the next generation?"

We still had much work to do, but we were on our way. We were not content just to wait for things to come back around.

APPLICATION

Waiting for Things to Come Back Around

Readings

Hear, O Israel: The LORD our God, the LORD is one. Love the LORD your God with all your heart and with all your soul and with all your strength. These commandments that I give you today are to be on your hearts. Impress them on your children. Talk about them when you sit at home and when you walk along the road, when you lie down and when you get up.

Deuteronomy 6:4–7

He took a little child whom he placed among them. Taking the child in his arms, he said to them, "Whoever welcomes one of these little children in my name welcomes me; and whoever welcomes me does not welcome me but the one who sent me."

Mark 9:36–37

APPLICATION

Waiting for Things to Come Back Around

Discussion Questions

1. Consider the positive impact that your church has had on your life and your community. How important is it to you personally that your church continue to have that kind of positive impact for future generations?

2. Generally, how do you think the average age of the people who attend your church compares with the average age of the people in your surrounding community? (The most recent census numbers can be helpful in answering this question.)

3. How confident do you feel that your church is effectively reaching (or will continue to effectively reach) the next generation—those who are younger than the average age of your community?

4. Which of these statements would people most likely hear you say?
   - "If it was good enough for me, it is good enough for our children."
   - "Let's do whatever it takes to reach the next generation."

5. Describe the differences in thoughts, words, and actions of a change agent compared to a change blocker. Which of these roles are you inclined to take on?

APPLICATION
Waiting for Things to Come Back Around

Action Planning

Strategy #1: Adopt a New Mindset

What practical actions can be taken to shift the mindset of the leaders and members of your church to genuinely embrace the question "What will it take to reach the next generation?"

Prayer

Father God, I come to you in Jesus' name. Help me (us) to fully and quickly adopt a mindset that, without compromising our core beliefs or values, we will do whatever it takes to reach the next generation with the life-changing message of Jesus Christ.

CHAPTER 2

MISSING THE WHALE

When I was in my midforties, I went on a three-day scuba diving trip on the Great Barrier Reef off of northeast Australia. On one of my favorite dives, I was about eighty feet deep. The amount and variety of fish and coral were stunning. I spent most of my dive observing from a few inches away a family of clown fish swimming in and around a large anemone. They were beautiful.

When I came to the surface and got back on deck, I wasn't surprised that the other divers were also excited about the dive. But I was surprised by *how* excited they were. When I asked why they were so enthusiastic, one diver said, "Didn't you see the whale?" Apparently, a dwarf minke whale swam right above us—I was the only one who didn't see it. I was so focused on the family of clown fish that I missed the whale.

> We spend our time focusing on so many good things that we lose sight of the most important reason our church exists.

Sometimes we are like that in our churches. We spend our time focusing on so many good things that we lose sight of the most important reason our church exists.

IDENTITY CRISIS

What is the whale for your church? What is your church's primary purpose for existing? What is the one thing around which everything else should revolve? In *Divine Renovation*, James Mallon writes, "I contend that our deepest crisis is an identity crisis, and that these other crises are but symptoms of this deepest crisis of all: we have forgotten who we are and what we are called to do as a Church. When this happens, we soon forget not only what our buildings are for, but why we exist as a Church to begin with."[1]

Missing the whale is not unique to churches. Organizations of any kind can easily lose sight of the most important reason for their existence. After researching organizations that had a long and steady track record of success, Jim Collins and Jerry I. Porras document their conclusions in their book *Built to Last*. They write, "Contrary to popular wisdom, the proper first response to a changing world is not to ask, 'How should we change?' but rather to ask, 'What do we stand for and why do we exist?' This should never change. And then feel free to change everything else."[2]

No matter how many programs and ministries churches may try to implement and keep alive, churches exist primarily as places for people to develop a genuine, life-changing faith in Jesus Christ. Many churches operate programs that mirror what other organizations already do while neglecting to focus on the one thing that no other organization can do. In *Courageous Leadership*, Bill Hybels puts it this way:

Businessmen can provide sorely needed jobs. Wise educators can teach useful knowledge of the world. Self-help programs can offer effective methods of behavior modification. Advanced psychological techniques can aid self-understanding. And all of this is good. But can any of it truly transform the human heart?

I believe that only one power exists on this sorry planet that can do that. It is the power of the love of Jesus Christ, the love that conquers sin and wipes out shame and heals wounds and reconciles enemies and patches broken dreams and ultimately changes the world, one life at a time. And what grips my heart every day is the knowledge that the radical message of that transforming love has been given to the church.

That means that in a very real way the future of the world rests in the hands of local congregations like yours and mine.[3]

> **Many churches operate programs that mirror what other organizations already do while neglecting to focus on the one thing that no other organization can do.**

CLARIFYING OUR VISION

At Amplify Church we had somehow lost sight of why we existed. We had become a church that was primarily about trying to *keep* the dwindling number of people who were still attending rather than trying to *reach* people in our community—including the next generation—who were not attending our church or any other church. The expenditure of time, energy, and resources on keeping people instead of reaching people had to change dramatically if the church was to have any chance of becoming the church that God created us to be.

I knew that many successful organizations use vision statements to help keep people in the organization from missing the whale, so I considered revising our church vision statement. Typically, a mission statement describes why an organization exists while a vision statement points to a desired future state. Whether you refer to the whale for your church as your church's vision or your church's mission, clarifying the "one thing" the people of your church embrace as their core identity is important.

I felt that a clear and compelling vision statement could be a powerful tool for directing and redirecting the way we were spending our time, energy, and resources at Amplify Church. This was especially true for us since we had obviously lost our way.

A powerful and effective vision statement must have these four characteristics:

1. Clear. No one wonders what it means.

2. Concise. It is short enough to fit on a T-shirt.

3. Inspiring. It resonates deeply with people in the organization.

4. Useful. It is worded in a way that helps to provide direction and shape decision making.

On May 25, 1961, President John F. Kennedy spoke these words: "I believe that this nation should commit itself to achieving the goal, before this decade is out, of landing a man on the moon and returning him safely to the earth." While this statement was not intended to represent the overall vision of our nation, it certainly was a clear, concise, inspiring, and useful vision statement about setting and reaching a goal that changed the world. On July 20, 1969, Neil Armstrong and Buzz Aldrin landed on the moon in the Apollo 11 lunar module. Along with command module pilot Michael Collins, they returned safely to earth four days later. What was thought to be impossible became a reality—a reality that was ignited by a statement of vision.

Our church's vision was not clear. It was not concise. It was so long that it would not have fit on a size XXL T-shirt. Since almost no one in the church knew what it was, it could not be inspiring or useful. As the new senior pastor, I presented a vision statement for Amplify Church that our church board unanimously agreed to adopt:

To lead as many people as possible into a growing relationship with Jesus Christ.

This vision statement was inspired by the vision statement of North Point Community Church, but we added the words "as many . . . as possible." Somehow the people of our church had accepted as truth a statement that is popular with declining churches: "God is more concerned with quality than quantity." This led to complacency despite our rapidly declining attendance. The thinking was that even though we were losing people, at least those who remained were "high-quality" people.

Of course this attitude automatically categorized those who had left the church as low-quality people. It also categorized those who had never attended the church as low-quality people. One of the people who took exception to the new church vision statement said, "Those of us who are still left need to focus on our own spiritual growth and depth before we try to reach others." While I understood this person's point of view, I knew this way of thinking would mean that the church would never reach out because we would never get "deep" enough. Contrast this way of thinking with the apostle Paul who was sharing his faith within a few days of his conversion. Personal growth *and* reaching out to others must *both* be priorities for every Christian. They are parallel priorities that are not in competition with one another.

> Our church had accepted as truth a statement that is popular with declining churches: "God is more concerned with quality than quantity."

We quoted our new vision statement at every weekend service. And we still quote it at every service. I spoke often in weekend messages during the first two years after assuming the role of senior pastor about our new vision statement and its implications. And it was discussed in every staff and leadership meeting. It also appeared on every key church communication. Before long, anyone who attended the church for any period of time had it memorized.

In his book *The Advantage: Why Organizational Health*

Trumps Everything Else in Business, Patrick Lencioni writes about the importance of "overcommunicating" for clarity:

> The problem is that leaders confuse the mere transfer of information to an audience with the audience's ability to understand, internalize, and embrace the message that is being communicated. The only way for people to embrace a message is to hear it over a period of time, in a variety of different situations, and preferably from different people. That's why great leaders see themselves as Chief Reminding Officers as much as anything else. Their top two priorities are to set the direction of the organization and then to ensure that people are reminded of it on a regular basis.[4]

The wording of our vision statement was not what helped to spark our church transformation. It was what the words represented. We already were experiencing a rapidly changing mindset as a church about reaching the next generation, but we needed clear focus and direction. Our clear vision allowed us to make the difficult decisions about which programs, ministries, and practices were absolutely essential to start reaching people again.

STRATEGY #2: IDENTIFY THE ESSENTIALS

Paul was encouraging the Colossians to live focused lives when he wrote, "Set your minds on things above, not on earthly things" (Colossians 3:2). Unfocused people seldom live up to their potential. Our lack of focus as a church was one reason we were not living up to our potential.

The simplest way to observe our lack of focus at Amplify Church was by looking at the size of our weekly bulletin. If you accidentally dropped our church bulletin on the floor, it would take some time to pick up all of the pages. We had an amazing number of church services, meetings, programs, and ministries, all sustained by a very small number of dedicated church members.

Each one of these things—the services, meetings, programs, and ministries—demanded time, resources, attention, and energy. Most of them were accomplishing good things and none was harmful in and of itself. But when combined together, they had a devastating effect on our ability to achieve our vision. The common denominator of most of these programs was not their link to a unified vision but the fact that they took place in our church building.

> Unfocused people seldom live up to their potential. Our lack of focus as a church was one reason we were not living up to our potential.

Ironically, I had started many of these services, meetings, programs, and ministries decades earlier. As a young pastor, I was a "yes" person. I said yes to almost every good idea, often turning loose the person whose idea it was to make it happen. Now, years later, every service, meeting, ministry, and program we had started was another plate that we had to keep spinning. It was exhausting.

IDENTIFYING OUR "VISION ESSENTIALS"

The most beneficial outcome of having a clear and compelling vision is *organizational focus*—the ability to differentiate between the good things you *can* do and the best things you *should* do to fulfill your church vision. After prayerful consideration, we decided to focus nearly 100 percent of our time, energy, and resources on three things we believed would have the greatest impact on our ability to fulfill our vision: *the weekend service, small groups,* and *children's and youth ministry.*

We were tempted to stress the importance of these things without dealing with competing priorities. However, we knew that piling new things on top of an organization that is already unfocused only guarantees ineffectiveness and increased frustration. To really focus on these three things, we had to accept that we could no longer focus our time, energy, and resources on some other things that had been a part of the fabric of our church for many years.

THE WEEKEND SERVICE

The *weekend service* was in dire need of attention. People had stopped inviting family and friends to church because our weekend services were perceived to be boring or irrelevant or both—especially by visitors. Our new goal was to plan each service so that it would make a tangible difference in the life of each person in attendance. We knew that we could not count on people to attend our church out of obligation. We had to plan and conduct our services so that people would want to come and feel excited about bringing others with them.

We took on the challenge of building our weekend services around the dual purposes of challenging Christ followers *and* reaching people who were far from God. Some contend that you must choose either to equip disciples or to reach unchurched people. Given our vision, we felt we had no choice but to plan weekend services that did both. I knew we were on the right track when long-term Christians began to indicate that they were growing in their faith in a way they had not grown in many years. I also knew we were on the right track when people who were not Christ followers indicated that they felt welcomed and engaged when they were invited to church.

Although we had plenty of open chairs on Sunday mornings, we added a Saturday evening service that was identical to our Sunday morning service. Because of modern schedule conflicts with adults and children, Sunday mornings were not free for many people in our community. Instead of wringing our hands about the "good old days" when Sunday mornings were schedule-free so people could attend church, we just added another option. Doing so made it easier for people to invite others.

Our goal was that the Saturday evening and Sunday morning services would be identical. The same musicians were required to play both weekend services, and they played the same songs. The same person shared the message at both services. The same children's programs were in full operation for both services. Once people knew that it was not a second-rate experience, Saturday evening church became a popular option.

Approximately one-third of our weekend attendees started to attend Saturday evening service.

We intentionally chose not to do two different *types* of services each weekend. Some people encouraged us to continue conducting the "traditional" service to which current members were accustomed and to just add a separate "contemporary" service. While this approach has worked well for some churches, we discovered that many churches that attempted to conduct two different types of services each weekend found that the effectiveness of one or both was compromised due to stretched resources. We had to be honest. We knew that we barely had enough time, energy, and resources to do one service well, much less two different types of services.

To make our weekend services as engaging as possible, we ended a tradition that had been a part of our church for over twenty years—the midweek service that had been conducted on Wednesday evenings. Even though the midweek service was never given the time and attention the weekend service received, it still took time and attention away from our preparation for the weekend. Since the midweek service was not identified as one of our three "vision essentials," we ended it.

While we received complaints from those who enjoyed attending church on Wednesday night, this decision removed a significant burden from worship team members and volunteers. It also made a big difference in the preparation time available for weekend messages in all of our environments, which improved the quality of the weekend messages. The increased focus on our weekend services resulted in every weekend service becoming a special service—one that was not to be missed.

SMALL GROUPS

In addition to the weekend services, we focused on building a strong small-group program. We felt that small groups were a critical part of helping people to build community and experience a growing relationship with Jesus Christ. The combination of Bible study and prayer in small groups would build meaningful connections for people with God and each other that could not be built solely during weekend services. I spent a fair amount of time sharing a vision for the impact that small groups could have on our church and encouraging people to give them a try. Since small groups were identified as a "vision essential," we made them a central part of who we were and are as a church.

Churches with effective small group programs tend to evaluate and reevaluate their approach on a regular basis, knowing that what works well for one church may not work well for another church—and that the approach that worked last year may not work as well this year. Our small group program has evolved over the years, and it now has a few features that have made it successful for our church:

1. *Church located.* We chose to locate our small groups in the church instead of in homes. We did this because we found that, for the most part, new people in our church were more apt to attend a small group at the church than to visit a stranger's home. They found it easier to come to the church building, at least initially. This meant that we needed to expand the spaces available for groups to meet. All of us on staff sacrificed our offices, which were transformed along

with several other rooms into "living room" environments with couches and comfortable chairs. We moved our offices to a remote location in our building that was not being used. Eventually we may need to have at least some home-based groups, but church-located groups have worked out well for us. They allow us to provide free child care in our children's ministry environments, an important service to our growing number of parents with young children. Currently our small group rooms are in use almost every night of the week.

2. *Core curriculum plus options.* Curriculum is not an afterthought. We spend a lot of time identifying a "core" curriculum each year that most of our small groups use. This brings unity to our efforts. Each year, the core curriculum is comprised of in-depth studies of various biblical books or biblical topics that are provided by excellent organizations such as InterVarsity Press, North Point Resources, and the Willow Creek Association. We installed DVD players in all of our small group rooms so we could use the growing number of video-based small group study options. As an option to the core curriculum, people can choose studies on specialized topics such as marriage, parenting, and financial management.

3. *Summer break.* Our initial attempts at having year-round small groups never worked. Every summer we had paltry and inconsistent attendance, so we decided to give all of our small groups a break for the summer. This break allows us to relaunch every September and results in renewed energy and enthusiasm. Every church has its own natural cycle, of course. We just found that it made sense for us to give people a chance to take a summer break from the weekly small group schedule.

4. *New groups each year.* We have found it best to have everyone sign up for a new group every fall. New friends are made every year in small groups, and no one has to be afraid of getting "stuck" in a group that stays together indefinitely. Although people can request to keep meeting with those with whom they have developed strong connections, we have found that every group in our church that insisted on staying together year after year eventually ended up with problematic relationships. Some of these problems could have easily been avoided if the group members had let go of their insistence to stay together.

5. *"Closed" groups.* Small groups at Amplify Church are not promoted as a place to invite unchurched people or friends who attend other churches. This allows group members to build a growing relationship with Jesus Christ by studying the Bible with other committed Christ followers from the same church. It also allows people to build closer relationships with others in their group while strengthening their commitment and increasing their passion for what is happening in our church.

6. *Monthly "Connect or Serve" Week.* We believe that it is important for our groups to do more than study and pray together. We want them to be engaged in relationship-building activities as well, including activities related to community service. Each month, one week of meeting time is devoted to an event that is focused on group connection or service. A typical connection event for a small group involves having dinner together at a member's home or restaurant. Serve events allow group members to volunteer together at an organization that is making a difference in the lives of hurting people in our

city and community. It has been extremely encouraging to see the impact that small groups have had by serving our larger community. In some aspects, our small groups are missional in the ways they serve as the hands and feet of Christ outside of the walls of our church.

Our small group leaders are not required to be Bible scholars. We train them to be effective facilitators and try to make sure that we provide them with materials that will set them up for success. These leaders are the backbone of our church because they provide much of the pastoral care needed by the people in their small group. They contact our church staff when a member is facing a particularly difficult issue, but they are the ones on the front lines praying for their small group members, encouraging them, and sometimes visiting them in times of need. This kind of attention is possible because our small groups are limited in size to approximately sixteen people.

To make sure that our small group program received the necessary focus, we ended some traditions that were a part of our church for many years. Given the increasingly hectic schedules of the people we were trying to reach, we felt that encouraging one church activity per week in addition to weekend services was challenging enough. We found that most people could not handle more activities or events than this.

We therefore had to make the difficult decision to end our Sunday school program. We did not end the program because we did not value the positive aspects of adult Sunday school classes. We simply felt that we could not do both Sunday school *and* small group ministry effectively. All of our Sunday school teachers were encouraged to become small group leaders, and all Sunday school attendees were encouraged to attend a small group.

We also merged our men's ministry and women's ministry into our small group program. We introduced small groups for men and small groups for women, limiting larger men's or women's events to annual events instead of planning programming on a weekly or monthly basis. As with any change, people who loved Sunday school or men's ministry or women's ministry in their former format were not excited about this change. Still, to my recollection, the only person who left the church over this change did so because our small groups were limited in size and this person wanted to have a bigger platform for her teaching ministry.

We found it very encouraging to hear stories of people praying for one another and supporting one another in our new small groups. As our dying church started to grow in attendance, people told us that their small groups were essential in keeping them connected in personal relationships. High-impact weekend services coupled with high-impact small groups led to tangible, positive changes in people's lives.

CHILDREN'S AND YOUTH MINISTRY

Although there were some challenges in refocusing our resources and energy on the weekend services and small groups, the greatest challenge of our renewed focus was in the area of *children's and youth ministry*. First, we added a new staff member and reassigned another staff person so that we now had both a children's director and a youth director. Even though these individuals were modestly paid and covered other areas of responsibility, adding these staff positions was a major commitment for our church at that time. One church member understandably asked, "Why do we need a children's director and a youth director when we have no children or youth?" I responded that without significant changes we would never see significant progress toward our future goals.

We purchased the best children's and youth curriculum we could find. The best fit for our church was curriculum from The reThink Group. We paid for our children's director and several key volunteers to attend the annual Orange Conference where they would be trained on how to maximize the impact of the new curriculum. Although the curriculum and conference costs stretched our budget, we knew that we couldn't afford not to invest in these things.

WE NO LONGER LIVE IN A *CAPTAIN KANGAROO* WORLD

The most significant change we made in our children's and youth ministry was the creation of new environments designed specifically for these age groups. We had a large church facility, but we had no dedicated space for children or youth. Every room in our building was "multipurpose," and our children and youth were able to use the rooms only when other activities and programs were not scheduled.

Our first attempt at creating new, dedicated space for children and youth was turning our chapel into a kids' theater, a room that resembled a studio for a children's television program. Because the chapel had been used by various adult church programs and ministries for many years, this change was controversial. One person said to us, "We don't need any designated areas for children—especially something that looks like a Disney stage. There are hardly any children in our church anyway. Just let them use adult spaces when we don't need them."

We also turned our gymnasium space into an amazing room where our middle school and high school students could meet. The room has a curtain that, when closed, allows the room to also be used for weddings, funerals, and other "adult" events, so it has some limited use as a multipurpose space. Still, the highest priority in the redesign of this space was our goal of reaching our youth. Along with this, we transformed other areas into colorful, high-impact spaces where preschool and elementary-aged children meet during adult church.

As you can imagine, with all of this change, there was a debate about how much we should invest in creating these "irresistible environments" for our children and youth. This is where our strategy of adopting a new mindset became critical. We had to think in terms of what it would take to reach our children instead of falling back to our natural response of "If it was good enough for me, it is good enough for our children."

> **We had to think in terms of what it would take to reach our children instead of falling back to the natural response of "If it was good enough for me, it is good enough for our children."**

When I was a child, the most stimulating thing about our Sunday school class was the flannel board the teacher used to teach us Bible stories. At the time, the flannel board was great. It wasn't all that different from the props used on the most exciting children's program on television at the time—*Captain Kangaroo*. We need to realize, however, that we no longer live in a *Captain Kangaroo* world; we live in a Disney and Nickelodeon world. Times have changed, and so must the way we connect with our children and youth.

FOCUS BECAME THE NORM

One of the positive results of learning to focus on our "vision essentials" was the increased confidence it brought to sharpen our focus in other areas such as missions. For years the church had been making modest contributions to many different organizations around the world. Like many churches, we had a world map with colored pins to indicate places we were sending support, even if a pin represented a few dollars of support each year.

Instead of continuing our broad but shallow approach to funding missions, we narrowed our focus to four places in the world where we had close, personal connections and where we could make a significant impact—Pittsburgh, India, Uganda, and Haiti. We began to partner with a number of organizations in the Pittsburgh area, including food banks, a ministry to the homeless, a ministry to single mothers, and a mentoring program for urban youth. We not only invested money into these organizations, but our small groups commonly devoted their "serve" weeks to these ministries, which were and are making a difference in our city. We increased our support of a ministry that plants churches in India. We also began to contribute a significant amount per month to support an orphanage for girls in Haiti.

Perhaps the biggest impact of this focused approach to missions came through a new partnership with Compassion International in Mukono, Uganda. Our church members started to sponsor over three hundred children in the neighborhoods around the Compassion International Child Development Center in Mukono. These children were cared for by an excellent church in that community, and our congregation gave enough to build a "piggery" (a shelter where pigs are raised) to help the families of the children we sponsored. We funded the construction of a library and training center to provide vocational skills to the children at the Child Development Center. We also gave enough to build a hatchery where chickens are raised to help the sponsored children's families.

The journey that led to our rewarding partnership with Compassion International started with our church youth group. The youth group decided to sponsor several children through Compassion International by pooling their part-time job earnings and allowances. Their efforts inspired the adults in our church to give and invest as well. Young adults are drawn to churches that make issues of poverty and social justice a priority. These things should be important to all of us, of course, but it is a particularly strong passion for those in the next generation. The practical result was that our efforts to become a new generation church led to significant increases in our missions budget.

I THINK THEY LIKE KIDS AROUND HERE

There was nothing easy about the changes we made to achieve our new focus on the weekend services, small groups, and children's and youth ministries, but it was worth all of the pain and effort when we began to see the results. It wasn't too long before people started to invite friends, family, and neighbors to church again, and attendance at our weekend services started to noticeably rise. In addition, over 50 percent of those attending weekend services started to regularly attend small groups.

Most exciting of all, we began to hear the sound of children in the halls of our church again. I remember two comments that confirmed to me that we were on the right track. I asked one man in his forties why he and his wife had started to attend Amplify Church even though they had not been affiliated with any church for many years. He told me that their teenage daughter had invited them. I was equally thrilled to overhear an elementary school child say to his parents during their first visit to our church, "I think they like kids around here."

When children and young adults started coming to our church again, it was very exciting. When we started to witness the life-changing power of Jesus Christ in people of all ages, it was beyond exciting. We missed some of the programs and ministries that had ended, but we knew that by focusing our time, energy, and resources on the truly essential things, our vision was becoming a reality. We were determined that we would never miss the whale again.

APPLICATION

Missing the Whale

Readings

We will not hide these truths from our children; we will tell the next generation about the glorious deeds of the LORD, about his power and his mighty wonders. For he issued his laws to Jacob; he gave his instructions to Israel. He commanded our ancestors to teach them to their children, so the next generation might know them—even the children not yet born—and they in turn will teach their own children. So each generation should set its hope anew on God, not forgetting his glorious miracles and obeying his commands.

Psalm 78:4–7 NLT

"What do you think? If a man owns a hundred sheep, and one of them wanders away, will he not leave the ninety-nine on the hills and go to look for the one that wandered off? And if he finds it, truly I tell you, he is happier about that one sheep than about the ninety-nine that did not wander off. In the same way your Father in heaven is not willing that any of these little ones should perish."

Matthew 18:12–14

APPLICATION
Missing the Whale

Discussion Questions

1. What is the "whale" for your church—your core mission and the primary reason you exist?

2. What indicators are there, if any, that your church may be more focused on *keeping* the people who already attend more than *reaching* people, including the next generation?

3. How would you respond if your church stopped doing some things that are personally important to you in order to more effectively focus on things that are deemed to be most critical to fulfilling the church vision?

4. What could be done to make the children's and youth ministry at your church irresistible both now and in the future?

APPLICATION
Missing the Whale

Action Planning

Strategy #2: Identify the Essentials

List the essential things on which your church should focus to make sure that your church's core mission continues into the next generation.

Prayer

Father God, I come to you in Jesus' name. Help me (us) to clearly see the things on which we as a church should focus our time, energy, and resources to best achieve the vision that you have given us.

CHAPTER 3

BARKING DOGS

Several years ago I met an elderly pastor of a storefront church with about a dozen members. After talking with him, I soon understood at least one reason why his church never grew much larger. He told me that he would take his dog with him to church every week, and the dog would lie down in front of the podium and frequently bark during the service. The regular attendees got used to having the pastor's beloved pet in church, but a visitor mentioned to him that the barking dog was a distraction. The pastor told me that he responded, "My dog is my best friend, and he stays even if that means you don't."

> Most churches have their share of barking dogs—things that distract members and visitors from the church's mission.

Most churches have their share of barking dogs—things that distract members and visitors from the church's mission. Dealing with the barking dogs of your church is touchy business because dogs are beloved creatures, part of the family. Most of us have become so accustomed to the barking dogs that we don't even notice their presence, but as soon as someone suggests getting rid of them, we grow upset or angry.

In his book, *Jesus Is _____*, Judah Smith writes about the extensive outreach campaign that City Church in Seattle put together to get the people of their city thinking and talking about the person and message of Jesus Christ. "Within months of launching the campaign, we realized something. Jesus Is _____ was more than a clever campaign or a marketing mantra. It was the mission of our church. A giant chalkboard in our church lobby now reads, 'Our mission: to show you who Jesus is.'"[1]

I love the passion behind their campaign. The people of City Church wanted to help people look beyond their misperceptions and see Jesus for who he really is. Isn't that a goal that every church shares? Unfortunately, most of our churches are filled with things that get in the way. While we cannot eliminate every distraction or barrier or "barking dog," we can try to reduce them and limit their impact.

ELIMINATING GOOD THINGS

We all know that there are times in our lives when we need to eliminate good things—even things that we like—from our schedules so that we can focus our time and energy on the most important things. The same principle is true for churches. Time, energy, and resources that we invest into unnecessary programs or ministries are time, energy, and resources that cannot be invested in the things that will directly fulfill God's vision for our church and have an impact on our ability to reach the next generation. To use an analogy, think of your church as a hot-air balloon. Some programs, ministries, and practices are like bags of sand that will have to be jettisoned if you are ever going to soar.

Because someone champions, nurtures, or defends them, some church programs and ministries continue to exist long after they should have ended. These guardians come by their love honestly. The program they champion may have once had a positive impact, and it may still be having some positive impact. But we need to exercise wisdom and discernment regarding when our church programs and ministries have run their course.

In their book *Simple Church*, researchers Thom S. Rainer and Eric Geiger help us put church programs into their proper perspective:

> **Think of your church as a hot-air balloon. Some programs, ministries, and practices are like bags of sand that will have to be jettisoned if you are ever going to soar.**

"Programs were made for man, not man for programs. If the goal is to keep certain things going, the church is in trouble. The end result must always be about people. Programs should only be tools."[2]

And Reggie Joiner, founder of The reThink Group, adds: "Your programs are not sacred. . . . What is sacred is the mission of the church. You are called to shine a light and demonstrate God's love and grace to those who need it. Our mission is not to preserve the local church as it presently exists in its various forms or models; our mission is to be the church. . . . All along [God] has planned this thing called the church so we could send a collective message to a generation that needs to know Him."[3]

What about your church? Chances are you have programs, ministries, and practices that should be eliminated. They are not bad things. They exist because they have accomplished or are accomplishing some good. But you may need to eliminate some *good* things because they are competing with and distracting you from the *best* things for your limited time, resources, and energy.

STRATEGY #3: REDUCE THE DISTRACTIONS

The writer of Hebrews speaks wisely about laying aside distractions: "Let us throw off everything that hinders and the sin that so easily entangles. And let us run with perseverance the race marked out for us" (Hebrews 12:1). We can understand how sinful things can be a distraction—sin entangles us and keeps us from running the race that God has marked out for us. But discerning when good things have become a distraction is far more difficult.

In 2003 Amplify Church was filled with barking dogs. Some of them were major distractions and some were minor. All of them had a negative impact on our vision *to lead as many people as possible into a growing relationship with Jesus Christ.* Our leadership team determined to look at our church with fresh eyes. We became detectives, working together to try to identify and eliminate as many distractions as possible.

Our conviction was that every distraction we eliminated could open the door wider to the people we were trying to reach, including the next generation. We were realistic enough to know that the elimination of some things that we deemed to be distractions would result in some people becoming upset. People are highly protective of their dogs no matter how loudly they bark. Nevertheless, we decided to take the risk.

In his book *Deep and Wide*, Andy Stanley writes about the importance of being willing to let go of things no matter how meaningful they have been in the past.

Nothing is new or innovative forever. Your best idea, the one that other churches emulate and take credit for, will eventually go the way of handbells and bus ministries. It's naïve and arrogant to think otherwise. We are foolish to assume that our ideas are transgenerational. We are equally foolish to assume that we will intuitively be able to sniff out the need for change in our own organizations. If it were that easy, everybody would have made the proper transitions at the proper time. Truth is, the clock is ticking on our good ideas. It's ticking backward. And it's ticking faster than we think.[4]

As you read about the things we eliminated at Amplify Church, you may think we went too far. We may have eliminated things that would not be appropriate for you to eliminate in your church; and what worked for us in our context and setting may not work for you. You may choose to focus on different priorities and thereby eliminate different distractions. That being said, I hope that our decisions will provoke you to think broadly: what things *should* you eliminate that are real or potential distractions

It is highly unlikely that every program, ministry, and practice in your church should continue to exist in perpetuity.

to your ability to fulfill your God-given vision? It is highly unlikely that every program, ministry, and practice in your church should continue to exist in perpetuity.

FIRST IMPRESSIONS

Visitors' first impressions color their entire perception of who you are as a church. We had a lot of things that fit under the category of "first impressions" that were barking dogs to our visitors. These had to change because they were distractions.

For example, the **small wooden sign at the church entrance** was rotting from weather and age. Anyone who saw it would assume that our church building was probably deteriorating as well. We covered the old sign with a canvas sign created by a local printer until we could afford a more modern and attractive sign.

Our **parking lot** consisted of gravel and dirt. Members knew not to wear nice shoes to church, but guests often started their experience at our church with muddy shoes or broken heels. This made a bad impression on people before they even entered our building. We sold some property that was no longer needed and used the proceeds to pave our parking lot.

A high **radio relay tower** rose from the top of the church roof. An attempt had been made to hide the radio tower by attaching to it a glittery silver cross. I do not know if the radio tower had anything to do with the leaks in our roof; I just knew that this monstrosity and the glittery cross that was bolted to it had to go. The owner of the tower was told to remove it within thirty days.

Our **church foyer** definitely influenced the first impressions of visitors to our church. The foyer was painted mauve, the same color it had been for more than a decade. Though it was the color of Pepto-Bismol, it had the opposite effect on visitors. We painted everything that was mauve a neutral shade of gray.

Bulletin boards lined the walls of the foyer and halls. On these bulletin boards, *anyone* could place *anything* they wanted, from business cards to flyers advertising programs in other churches. Many of the things posted were outdated. The sheer volume of information hanging on these bulletin boards screamed to visitors that we were an unfocused church. All of the bulletin boards were removed, and relevant current information was placed in our newly formatted one-page bulletin and on our website.

The meeting rooms right off of the foyer contained **outdated and used furniture** that members had donated. These rooms looked like a grandmother's parlor. All of the hand-me-down furniture was removed. We also removed the mismatched end tables in our sanctuary that were topped with plastic plants and tissue boxes.

The sanctuary contained a combination of **aging green pews and stained rust-colored chairs**. There were so few people left in the church that everyone could choose their seat each weekend. Some people gravitated to their favorite green pew. Others chose to sit in the rust-colored chairs with the fewest stains. It took some time, but eventually we replaced both of these options with modern individual seating.

CHURCH PROGRAMS AND MINISTRIES

For several reasons, we chose to end the **evangelism training program** that had been conducted for over twenty years at the church. This program required people to attend a class weekly for several months to receive an evangelism certificate. One reason we ended this program was that it was competing with small groups, one of our new priorities. Few people could attend both. In addition, the format of the program created an impression for some that the responsibility to evangelize or even invite others to church was primarily carried by those who were "certified." We didn't want to communicate that to our members.

We asked the people who ran the **food bank** that was located in the church to move to a new location. The vast majority of the people who were served by the food bank lived in a neighboring community. I found out that the leaders in a church in that community had been praying about starting a food bank, so we talked to them and moved the food bank to that church. The number of people served by this ministry increased significantly. We have since supported that food bank with volunteers and monthly financial support. This decision opened up much-needed space for our growing youth ministry.

We asked a **drug rehab program** that was meeting in our chapel to relocate to another church. The leaders of the program, who did not attend our church, found another church that was pleased to house them. The program continued as strong as ever, and this decision allowed us to transform the chapel they had been using into the kids' theater.

The decision that freed up the most space for our children's and youth ministry was closing the **K-12 Christian school** that had been sponsored by and housed in our church. Severe financial pressures the school was facing due to declining enrollment influenced this decision. But it was still a very difficult decision since the school had provided quality Christian education for hundreds of students for almost twenty years.

One benefit that resulted from the school closing was the elimination of the constant conflicts between the school and the church over how to best utilize the building. One school parent who did not attend Amplify Church told me, "This building belongs to the school, and the church just has to work around us." Another school parent said, "If your church children are in one of our classrooms on the weekend, everything on Monday better be exactly as it was on Friday—or else." The tail was truly wagging the dog.

The closure of the school changed my personal focus as well. Having a parent call me with a request to intervene with a teacher in the school because her child had received a B instead of an A on a test was not unusual. The time that I had been devoting to resolving problems at the school was now freed up to better focus on advancing the vision of our church.

CHURCH PRACTICES

Our church had adopted a number of practices over the years that we felt were potential distractions or barriers to reaching people, including the next generation. We eliminated some practices that gave our church a **sense of formality** that I felt was less appropriate than it was in the past. We ended the unwritten formal dress code that had been a part of the church since its inception. Because of relaxed dress codes in the workplace and schools, a significant percentage of young men did not even own a suit. Though wearing a suit to church was not required, visitors could readily see that only formal dress was acceptable. This was a barrier to visitors, especially younger people.

Also, in an effort to reduce the formality of my relationship with the congregation, I made it clear that I would not be offended if adults called me Lee instead of Pastor Lee or Reverend Kricher. We eliminated reserved parking spaces for staff, and we removed the large, throne-like chair on the platform that the pastor sat on during the service. I began to sit with the congregation at weekend services until it was time for me to share the message. These were small changes, but together they helped to change the culture of our church.

We moved **prayer requests** from the weekend service to small groups, which were being attended by a growing number of people. Reading and praying for an untold number of prayer requests during weekend services was a huge distraction. The congregation heard each request in detail twice—once when it was read out loud and once when prayers were offered. Some of these requests were stunningly remote, such as "My aunt Janice from Colorado has a neighbor whose dog is suddenly urinating inside of the house and they can't figure out why. Please pray for wisdom." I could tell that both members and visitors were having a hard time staying engaged during our congregational prayers—particularly visitors who didn't know anyone we prayed for.

Another practice that we eliminated was the distribution of **voter guides**. Traditionally these had been passed out for several weeks prior to each election. The candidates endorsed in these guides were typically pro-life candidates, and the need to vote for pro-life candidates was reinforced by a large poster of a fetus that greeted people when they entered the main entrance. The message to visitors was unmistakably clear: *You do not belong in this church unless you vote pro-life.* We took down the poster and stopped the distribution of voter guides. These actions were not at all because of a change in the personal convictions of our church members. They were just an indication that we had a higher priority than leading as many people as possible to vote for pro-life candidates—we had the priority *to lead as many people as possible into a growing relationship with Jesus Christ.*

Moreover, these actions stemmed from a broader decision that we would not confuse the message of Christ with a message for **political action**. Some church leaders feel that using their influence to rally people around their political convictions is important. I am not one of those leaders. Many of our members are very active in the political process, but we felt that calls for political action *as a church* could easily distract members and visitors from the primary reason we exist as a church. *Every church will need to navigate this tension carefully.* Even though many young adults are passionate about combating hunger, poverty, human slavery, and other types of global injustice, they tend to be put off by churches that are overtly political.

Certainly some people will be drawn to a church that is known to be a church for Republicans or a church for

Democrats, but in identifying this way, you are strategically choosing to discount a large percentage of the community you are called to serve. To keep myself accessible to a broad cross-section of our community, I purposely do not advertise my own political views from the pulpit. For example, after the most recent presidential election, a married couple asked me to settle a dispute. The husband thought I voted for the Democratic candidate, and the wife thought I voted for the Republican candidate. I was pleased to let them continue conjecturing.

UNIQUE PRACTICES

Every church has practices that are unique to that particular church. Church leaders often view the unique practices of other churches as bizarre, but they tend to be somewhat unaware of or blind to their own unique practices. Our church had been established in the late 1970s during the charismatic movement, and those charismatic roots were still evident in several of our practices. We had to decide which of these practices should be set aside because they were distractions to fulfilling our vision.

Church leaders often view the unique practices of other churches as bizarre, but they tend to be somewhat unaware of or blind to their own unique practices.

One of the practices we ended was the presence of an **open microphone** in the sanctuary during weekend services. Anyone in the church could walk up to this microphone during the service to share a testimony or a word of encouragement whenever they felt moved to do so. Sometimes it was just saying something like, "The Lord put the twenty-third Psalm on my heart this week, so I want to read it to all of you." Other times people spoke "prophetically" on behalf of God. This was often something encouraging, such as "The Lord says, 'I will be there for you when you are hurting because I love you.'" But sometimes it was confusing. One person shared, "The Lord says, 'It's okay to be afraid. Sometimes I'm afraid, too.'" I remember thinking that if God is afraid, we are all in big trouble. The open microphone was meaningful for some people who thought that it was proof that we were open to the spontaneous work of the Holy Spirit. For many others, though, this practice was a primary reason why they did not invite guests to our church.

We also ended what I call **"individual displays of worship."** While the congregation was singing, it was not unusual for individuals to leave their seats and express their worship while standing in an aisle or in the front of the church. They sometimes waved streamers, banners, or flags as part of their worship. I never questioned their sincerity, but I knew that visitors would be looking at these individuals instead of focusing on the meaning of the words of the songs that were being sung. So we instituted a new practice. People could sing, clap, or lift their hands as an expression of worship, but we asked them to remain at their seats. The streamers, banners, and flags were retired from service. Our new practice regarding worship was "Join in without standing out."

Another practice that we eliminated was the **prayer lines** at the conclusion of the service. Prayer lines formed when several church leaders stood in front of the congregation and, while quiet music played, people went to them individually for prayer. As you can imagine, these prayer lines extended our service times significantly. When people did leave before all of the prayers were completed, they had to leave quietly and had little interaction with others before exiting. We decided to make small groups the primary place where people received personal prayer rather than our weekend services. We scheduled small group leaders to be available in a designated prayer room after weekend services for those who did not attend a small group.

Some of you who come from different church traditions may be rolling your eyes about the unique practices we had in our church, but you probably have some unique practices in your church as well. These are things you have "always done" that you may not recognize as having a negative impact on your ability to fulfill your vision and reach the next generation. Don't simply assume that these unique practices are just "who you are." If they are a distraction to fulfilling your vision, you have to decide—are these things *really* an essential part of our identity as a church, or are they actually barking dogs?

NAME CHANGE

One of our biggest barking dogs was the name of our church. When I helped to found the church in the late 1970s, an organization that had become quite well known in many circles was the Full Gospel Businessmen. People from many types of churches attended Full Gospel Businessmen's meetings where they experienced contemporary worship music and an inspiring message. Because we were located in the eastern suburbs of Pittsburgh and because our church services were more like

Full Gospel Businessmen's meetings than traditional liturgies, we adopted the name *Pittsburgh East Full Gospel Church*. Most people knew what to expect just by hearing our name.

By 2003, Full Gospel Businessmen meetings were only remembered by a handful of aging members. In fact, when I asked people from our community what the name of the church meant to them, the most common response was that our name was an insult to other churches in the community whom we must consider to be "partial gospel churches." So we changed the name of the church to Pittsburgh East Community Church because we felt it would better help us to achieve our vision. Later, when we added two campuses that were not in the eastern suburbs of Pittsburgh, we adopted the name Amplify Church, which was not specific to any particular location. If changing the name of your church can help you to better fulfill your vision, you would be wise to make the change.

REACTING TO CRITICISM

With all of these changes came inevitable criticisms. Dealing with criticism can be highly distracting as well, so if your goal is to reduce distractions, you need to have a plan for how you will react to critics! We found that people were not upset about the identification of the essentials we needed to focus on to best achieve our vision. They were upset about the elimination of programs, ministries, and practices that were near and dear to them.

Some people told us that the relaxed dress code showed disrespect for God's presence. Others said that we did not care about unborn children because we stopped distributing pro-life voter guides. One person who had shared a testimony or word almost every weekend left the church when we eliminated the open microphone. Another who was popularly known as the "flag waver" left when we adopted our "join in without standing out" approach to expressions of worship. When the food bank moved to another church, some declared that we no longer cared about hungry people. When the drug rehab program moved to another church, others claimed that we no longer cared about people with drug problems. When the K–12 Christian school was closed, some people left the church saying that we no longer cared about Christian education.

I took every criticism personally when I was a young pastor—especially if people left the church as a sign of their displeasure. Now, as an older pastor, I took the criticism of our changes much more philosophically. I knew that some people would disagree with or be offended by one or more of the changes. After all, the changes were being made to aspects of the church that were meaningful to people. Those who stayed were taking a leap of faith that we would reach more people with our new approach to church. And those who left were not bad people or selfish "change resistors"; they just didn't personally resonate with the new direction we were taking. I was sad to see people leave over some of the changes we made, but I was convinced that without significant change, we would continue on our path of decline.

I went out of my way to show respect and understanding to those who were upset and to those who left. My goal was to explain the rationale for change and not criticize their resistance to it. I was determined to take the apostle Paul's advice to be at peace, as much as is possible, with all.

As far as I know, every person who left the church found another good church where they continued to worship and serve Christ. I recently saw a person who had been one of my biggest critics. We shook hands, and I expressed understanding of the concerns he had voiced. He expressed understanding about why we made the changes we made and expressed genuine happiness that the church was healthy and thriving again.

> I was determined to take the apostle Paul's advice to be at peace, as much as is possible, with all.

When you know that your motive is to do God's will and you are sincerely committed to God's best for the church and the community, you can respond without defensiveness and resentment to those who are critical of the changes taking place in your church. Take the high road, and try to be patient and gracious instead of defensive and resentful. How you treat the critics will serve as an example to those who believe in the changes. Moreover, your heart will be right with God at a time when you need to know his presence and seek his favor.

CHOOSING WHAT NOT TO DO

To sum up our approach, we simply put everything on the table—everything but our core beliefs and the vision God had given us for the future. We eliminated a lot of barking dogs that we felt were either major or minor distractions from the essentials we determined were most critical to fulfilling our vision. We also stopped introducing new programs, ministries, and practices that were not directly tied to our vision. Saying no to starting something new in a church is far easier than stopping something that has become a part of the life of the church.

I cannot state with confidence that every individual change we made had a significant impact on the revitalization of our church. However, I can state with confidence that, *collectively*, the changes we made did have a significant and positive impact on the revitalization of our church. Our members and visitors once again started to invite family, friends, and coworkers to come to church. We stopped hearing members say, "I don't invite others because they will think our church is boring," or "I don't invite others because they might think our church is weird," or "I don't invite others because new people feel like unwelcome outsiders when they visit our church."

When all is said and done, though, effectively fulfilling your vision is as dependent on what you choose not to do as it is on what you choose to do.

Your church's list of programs, ministries, and practices that need to be let go will likely be quite different from ours. Some churches that include many of the things we eliminated are thriving and reaching the next generation. When all is said and done, though, effectively fulfilling your vision is as dependent on what you choose not to do as it is on what you choose to do.

APPLICATION
Barking Dogs

Readings

Children are a heritage from the LORD, offspring a reward from him.

Psalm 127:3

He called a little child to him, and placed the child among them. And he said: "Truly I tell you, unless you change and become like little children, you will never enter the kingdom of heaven. Therefore, whoever takes the lowly position of this child is the greatest in the kingdom of heaven. And whoever welcomes one such child in my name welcomes me.

"If anyone causes one of these little ones—those who believe in me—to stumble, it would be better for them to have a large millstone hung around their neck and to be drowned in the depths of the sea."

Matthew 18:2–6

APPLICATION
Barking Dogs

Discussion Questions

1. What good things have you eliminated from your personal life or schedule in order to better focus your time and energy on the most important things? In what ways, if any, does this apply to your church?

2. Which first impressions, programs, ministries, or practices of your church are potential "barking dogs" that may be a minor or major distraction to fulfilling your vision and reaching the next generation?

3. Which church programs or ministries are you most highly invested in personally?

4. Which church program, ministry, or practice means so much to you that you would leave the church if it were to be discontinued?

APPLICATION
Barking Dogs

Action Planning

Strategy #3: Reduce the Distractions

List first impressions, programs, ministries, and/or practices in your church that could be a distraction to reaching the next generation.

Prayer

Father God, I come to you in Jesus' name. Help me (us) to have a teachable spirit so that I (we) will not react defensively to the idea that things may need to change in our church.

CHAPTER 4

SILVER VEGA

A few years after my wife, Linda, and I were married, we purchased a used car. We didn't have the money to buy a decent car, so we bought a used red Chevrolet Vega. There is a reason Chevrolet no longer makes the Vega. Words cannot describe how bad that car was.

Our Chevy Vega seldom started at the first turn of the key. When it finally did start, at forty miles per hour it would shake uncontrollably as if it were falling apart. The heating and ventilation system was terrible. But probably the worst part of our Vega was the body. New holes seemed to rust through that car every time I dared to look. It was a real mess.

Instead of spending the money to buy a different car, I came up with a better idea. I had the car painted silver—classic Mercedes silver. It looked a lot nicer. Unfortunately, the silver Vega was still the same car. It was now a silver piece of junk instead of a red piece of junk. We got rid of it a few months later.

You can't fix serious problems with a new coat of paint. That is true for an old car, and it is equally true for a church in decline. I have seen plenty of examples of this over the years. One church added a youthful touch to one weekend service per month by allowing one of their youngest regular attendees (a guy in his midforties) to lead a song while playing his acoustic guitar. Another church I know painted a colorful mural on the concrete wall of the dark basement room where the kids were sent each week. Still another church added an underfunded and understaffed "contemporary service" to the weekly calendar.

Unsurprisingly, none of these efforts succeeded. They failed because they were surface-level changes not supported by a passionate commitment to do whatever it takes to reach the next generation. They were examples of low effort that resulted in low impact. They were a testament to the fact that you can't reach the next generation by painting your Vega silver.

PURSUING EXCELLENCE

Jim Collins begins his classic book *Good to Great* with these words: "Good is the enemy of great. And that is one of the key reasons why we have so little that becomes great. We don't have great schools, principally because we have good schools. We don't have great government, principally because we have good government. Few people attain great lives, in large part because it is just so easy to settle for a good life."[1]

Given the tendency of organizations to become complacent, it is understandable that churches with stretched resources tend to conduct services, ministries, and programs in a way that no one would describe with the word *excellence*.

But if the church is the hope of the world, we cannot be satisfied with mediocrity. In his book *The Catalyst Leader*, Brad Lomenick challenges leaders to create an organization where excellence is nonnegotiable:

Capable leaders are willing to set standards that scare them. Ask yourself the question, 'Are you operating at good, better or best?' Good is doing what is expected of you. It is slightly above average and requires some focus and determination to get there, but it is relatively easy to achieve. Better is rising a little higher than good. It typically means you are comparing yourself to the next one in line. But best is where you want to live. It is greatness and doesn't mean you are better than everyone else but that you're working to your maximum capability.[2]

One pastor told me that he never attends conferences at churches that are accomplishing more than his church because he leaves feeling jealous and discouraged. I feel quite the opposite. I love visiting churches that are accomplishing more than our church. Instead of feeling jealous and discouraged, I feel challenged and inspired. I always leave determined to elevate things to a higher level in our church. So why do we experience things so differently? I believe his attitude and discomfort stem from a misunderstanding of what pursuing excellence is all about.

> **The pursuit of excellence is all about "minding the gap" ... between where you are as a church and where you have the potential to be. That is the gap you need to identify and close.**

In London's underground rail system, the phrase "Mind the gap" can be found painted along the edges of train platforms. This visual warning is issued with an identical audible warning so that passengers take caution when stepping across the spatial gap from the station platform onto the train.

The pursuit of excellence is all about "minding the gap." This is *not* the gap between your church and some other church. It is the gap between where you are as a church and where you have the potential to be. That is the gap you need to identify and close. In fact, you will never fulfill your God-inspired vision if you are satisfied leaving that gap as it is.

STRATEGY #4: ELEVATE YOUR STANDARDS

Paul wrote to the Corinthians, "But since you excel in everything—in faith, in speech, in knowledge, in complete earnestness and in the love we have kindled in you—see that you also excel in this grace of giving" (2 Corinthians 8:7). Elevating your standards is about aspiring to excel in everything you do. It is about closing the gap between where you are and where you have the potential to be.

Elevating your standards as a church is very difficult if your church is unfocused. You are juggling too many things to achieve excellence in anything. But once you identify the essentials and reduce your distractions, elevating the standards for what is left is very doable.

Pursuing excellence was an alien idea at Amplify Church. We had too many things going on with too little time and too few resources to give anything the attention that was needed to take it to a level that would engage the people we needed to reach. We had lived with a lack of excellence for so long that mediocrity had become acceptable.

One example was our website. Next to personal invitations, the primary way that people find out about your church is through your website. In 2003, our website looked like a flower-covered bulletin cover from the 1980s. It had some basic information, but it was formatted in a way that was uninspiring and unattractive. Anyone under fifty years old would have looked at our website and concluded that our church was a church for old people who did things in outdated ways. They would have been correct, of course, but we were changing. We contracted with a person who helped us create a new website that better represented who we felt God was calling us to be as a church. It was one sign that we were elevating our standards.

ELEVATING THE WEEKEND SERVICE

Your church's weekend services are perfectly designed to reach the people you are reaching. If you want to reach others, things need to change. At Amplify Church we were reaching people who were in their fifties and older who had attended our church for many years. We had to elevate the weekend service experience to reach people who weren't coming.

Your church's weekend services are perfectly designed to reach the people you are reaching. If you want to reach others, things need to change.

We changed a number of things that made it easier for our members to invite young adults to our church. Many of the same changes made it easier for members to invite older adults as well. Collectively, these changes were made with the hope of dramatically improving the experience that both members and visitors had when attending Amplify Church.

A small **creative team** was formed of staff and volunteers to prayerfully plan every weekend service. I let the creative team know which topics I planned to cover in my messages for the next three to six months. The creative team then planned several weeks in advance to determine how to best reinforce the themes of the upcoming weekend messages with graphics, videos, special music, takeaways, and other service elements. Every part of the experience visitors had—from their entrance to the parking lot to their exit—was discussed.

We added new **volunteer roles**. Parking lot attendants were the first smiling faces seen by visitors. Greeters were trained how to best welcome people as they entered the foyer and the sanctuary. "VIP Team" members welcomed first-time visitors.

The room adjacent to the foyer was turned into a **café**, something we knew many churches had done to encourage the kind of natural personal connections that occur over coffee. Before long, members started to arrive early and to bring guests. They were confident that their guests would have a positive impression of our church from the moment they came onto our church campus.

We made a simple change to our **preservice and postservice environment** inside the sanctuary. In a world where face-to-face connections are becoming rarer, we felt that the time before and after service should be filled with the energy that comes from people interacting with one another. We replaced silence and somber music with upbeat modern worship music. This gave people "permission" to spend time greeting their friends and meeting the new people who were starting to attend.

We also changed the **service length**. Church services at Amplify Church had been a minimum of ninety minutes and often longer. We decided to limit the length of the service to approximately sixty-five minutes. This was most appreciated during football season when the Pittsburgh Steelers had an early afternoon football game! People actually started to comment that they wished the services were longer. That was much preferred to the days when they were wishing the services were shorter.

One way we elevated the weekend service experience was by reducing the time devoted to **announcements**. People had become accustomed to the champions of each program or ministry getting up and rallying support for upcoming activities. It was not unusual for the announcements to take as long as thirty minutes, time that visitors of all ages found to be mostly irrelevant. The length of the announcements was reduced, of course, when most of the programs and ministries that had been highlighted during announcement time no longer existed. But we also adopted a policy that announcements had to be pertinent to the majority of people present, and this dramatically reduced announcement time.

We considered every element of the weekend service experience. We began to do **Scripture readings** from recent translations so that visitors would not be required to interpret the meaning of words that were no longer in common use. Also, the Scripture readings and the lyrics of worship songs were projected onto newly installed **video screens**. In this way, visitors had the same easy access to the words as regular attendees. We moved two crosses to adjacent walls so we could install the video screens. (That led to at least one person's departure from the church, saying, "Now they're moving the crosses!")

The bottom line is that the weekend service experience for members and particularly for visitors changed dramatically and resulted in dramatically increased attendance.

Some members thought that advanced planning for weekend services was inappropriate. They equated the work of the Holy Spirit with unplanned spontaneity. But a better indication of the work of the Holy Spirit is changed lives. The creativity and planning that we put into our weekend services led to a dramatic increase in attendance and a dramatic increase in the stories we heard about lives that were changed through faith in Jesus Christ.

ELEVATING THE MUSIC

Please skip this section if your blood pressure rises at just the thought of changing the musical style of your church. I must tread on this dangerous ground, though, because I believe that the changes we made to our style of music had a profound effect on our ability to reach the next generation.

I love music that reconnects me to my high school and college years. In the past few years, Linda and I have attended concerts by James Taylor, Chicago, the Beach Boys, the Rolling Stones, Diana Ross, Frankie Valli, and many other musical artists we started to listen to in high school and college. We enjoyed every concert, but we also marveled at how many old people were in attendance.

I never quite understood why our daughters didn't want to go to these concerts. I guess they don't relate to our music as much as I think they should. On the other hand, we don't attend the concerts that our daughters attend or relate to their music, either. Musical tastes change from generation to generation. Knowing the importance of music in all of our lives, each church must decide if its style of music will appeal primarily to those who are older or to those who are younger.

If musical style is one of the things that is "on the table" when considering changes in your church,

> **Knowing the importance of music in all of our lives, each church must decide if its style of music will appeal primarily to those who are older or to those who are younger.**

then it is wise to observe what musical styles are being played in churches that are most effectively reaching the next generation. In their book *Comeback Churches*, Ed Stetzer and Mike Dodson share conclusions about their research of three hundred formerly declining churches that experienced genuine revitalization:

> Comeback churches were more contemporary than traditional. Although we are not advocating that every church be contemporary, and many of the churches in our study were not, it would be inappropriate not to recognize the influence of contemporary worship. The vast majority of American churches are not contemporary; the majority in this study would seem to be, and that should make us take notice.[3]

In my observation, the musical style in the churches that were most effective at reaching young people appealed primarily to those who were younger. It had a current rather than a dated sound. Two of the leading sources for contemporary worship were (and are) Hillsong and Passion, with a sound and style quite different from what we had at Amplify Church.

In 2003, Amplify Church had music that was perfectly suited to the people who were attending. The song choices were primarily popular hymns and choruses that were the soundtrack for the spiritual lives of those who were in their fifties and above. The style of music was very meaningful to the regular attendees. Most could not understand why young people did not connect with our music.

The strength of emotion connected to the musical style at Amplify Church was evident in the response to two questions I asked our members during a weekend service. Inspired by a message I heard by Louie Giglio, founder of the Passion worship movement, I asked, "How many of you would give your right arm for your children or grandchildren?" Almost every hand went up. Then I asked, "How many of you would give up your music for your children or grandchildren?" Far fewer hands were raised.

We decided to change our style of worship and began utilizing a style exemplified by Hillsong and Passion, a more contemporary style. We were fortunate to be able to hire a young man who had attended Hillsong Leadership College who could serve as both our youth director and music director. He had a good understanding of the style of music we felt would reach a younger audience.

My own willingness to change despite my personal preferences was tested early on when the music director requested that we replace the grand piano with a synthesizer to better support our new style of music. He made this request with fear and trembling, knowing that I had personally handpicked our grand piano many years earlier, and it held a place close to my heart. But I approved his request. For a fraction of the cost we had paid for the grand piano, we purchased a new synthesizer for the sanctuary. The grand piano was moved to our worship team's practice room.

While I expected that changes to our worship style would be offensive to some people, I was not worried that changing our style of music would be offensive to God. These changes were changes of style, not content. Over the years, I had worshiped with a congregation that sang "Amazing Grace" in a traditional style accompanied by a solitary organ. I had worshiped with a congregation that sang "Amazing Grace" in an orchestral style accompanied by a piano and a small orchestra. I had worshiped with a congregation that sang "Amazing Grace" in a contemporary style accompanied by a rock band. In none of these situations was the genuineness of my worship determined by the style of the music. Styles change, but it is the heart of the worshiper that brings honor to God. In fact, I anticipate that the style of our music will continue to evolve in the decades to come as we seek to stay connected to coming generations.

MUSICAL EXCELLENCE

No matter what musical style you believe will best advance your vision, elevating the excellence of your music should be a priority. It only makes sense that you have a better chance of reaching new people if the music of your church would be described by an objective person as excellent.

At Amplify Church we held auditions for the worship team, and only singers and musicians with the musical skills that matched our musical goals were chosen. Prior to this, anyone who wanted to be on the worship team was welcome, no matter his or her level of musical expertise. Over twenty people auditioned, but only a few were chosen. Other talented singers and musicians were recruited, some of whom were former church members who were excited about the new direction of the church.

No matter what musical style you believe will best advance your vision, elevating the excellence of your music should be a priority.

One reason we raised the bar for our singers and musicians was because the songs we wanted to sing during weekend services were more musically complex than the songs we had been singing. Not only was a higher level of musical expertise required but also a much bigger commitment was required of singers and instrumentalists. Rehearsals entailed two to three hours on Wednesday evenings and two more hours before weekend services started. The practice paid off. Before long, the dramatic change in musical style was matched by a dramatic change in musical excellence.

We did not introduce these changes to our music incrementally over a long period of time. The change was immediate and sudden. One weekend every song was sung in the old style. The next weekend every song was sung in the new style. We had complaints about the change, of course. The most common complaint was about the volume of the music. We have had to continually balance the need for a volume level that matches the style of music with the need for a volume level that offends the fewest number of people. Free earplugs are made available at every service.

To indicate my personal support for the new style of worship, I made it a point to be present at the start of every service so I could worship with the congregation. I have attended churches where pastors are only visible immediately prior to the time they would speak. It gave me the impression that they saw the worship time only as an unimportant prelude to their message. I felt that worshiping with the congregation not only honored God but showed appreciation for the time and effort our worship team members put into every service because of their commitment to excellence.

In conjunction with our musical changes, we made major changes to our sanctuary to make young adults feel more excited about coming to adult church. We installed audio, video, and lighting components that complemented the new style of music. We also painted the sanctuary a darker color to make it more intimate than the bright white color it had been. All of these things together had a significant impact on the weekend service experience.

Some people chose to leave the church over the changes to our music, including most of those who auditioned for the worship team but were not chosen. But most people stayed and, even if they didn't like it initially, the new style of music grew on them. One long-term member told me, "I was not very happy with the changes in our music, but it was clear

We began to believe that the difficult changes were worth it when our new style and the excellence of our worship music became one of the primary reasons that new attendees gave for starting to attend Amplify Church.

that the words we were singing were biblical and God-honoring. I decided that is the most important thing." Another long-term member said, "Not only am I thrilled to see young people in our church, but this music is making me feel young again."

We began to believe that the difficult changes were worth it when our new style and the excellence of our worship music became one of the primary reasons new attendees gave for starting to attend Amplify Church.

ELEVATING THE MESSAGES

No matter how effectively parking lot attendants help people to park their cars, or how warmly the greeters welcome people, or how pleasant an environment you provide in your foyer, or how much the worship experience reflects musical excellence and sincerity—it all comes down to the message. If the pastor does not present a clear, compelling, and relevant message on a regular basis, your church will never become what God intends.

As a pastor, I didn't compare my speaking ability to the speaking ability of the great communicators I had heard in my life. I knew that God did not expect me to try to be someone else. However, I also knew that there was a sizable gap between who I was as a communicator and who I could be as a communicator. I knew that I had to do whatever it would take to close that gap.

When I was a young pastor, I did not take my weekend messages seriously enough. If I had a busy week, I just did what I thought I could do, even if that meant pulling out a message that I had done before and updating it a bit. I used three-point or four-point or five-point messages, hoping that at least one of the points would be helpful to someone listening.

My thoughts about weekend messages changed during the years I was not in pastoral ministry. I traveled extensively and often worked more than sixty hours a week. Every minute of every weekend at home was precious. If I was going to spend time on a Sunday morning driving to and from church and sitting in a church service, I expected the message to make a tangible difference in my life. I know that some people call that a "consumer mentality," but I wanted church to have a positive impact on my life and on the lives of the family members and friends who came with me.

When I returned to full-time ministry, considering the twenty-five to thirty minutes each weekend that I would be speaking was sobering. Dozens and eventually hundreds of people were spending their weekend hours at church. When I multiplied those twenty-five to thirty minutes by the number of people in attendance, I felt a tremendous responsibility to elevate my messages. I knew that would not happen without a lot of work.

In his book *Preaching: Communicating Faith in an Age of Skepticism*, Tim Keller notes that the work of the Holy Spirit is the main difference between good and great preaching. Yet he is also clear about the hard work that such preaching requires: "Understanding the biblical text, distilling a clear outline and theme, developing a persuasive argument, enriching it with poignant illustrations, metaphors, and practical examples, incisively analyzing heart motives and cultural assumptions, making specific application to real life—all of this takes extensive labor."[4]

Elevating my weekend messages became my highest priority. I began to spend at least half of my work week in preparation for the weekend message—often twenty-five hours or more. This was made possible only by communicating to the congregation that I would not be doing all of the hospital visits, counseling, weddings, and funerals. I identified others who could share the load and coached them so they would be successful. I applied to my personal schedule the same principles of focus that we were applying as a church. One thing that helped tremendously was that we minimized the number of meetings that took place in our church. The number of church board meetings and staff meetings were significantly less than when the church was much, much smaller.

Setting aside the extensive time needed to elevate my weekend messages was just part of the equation. I also had to choose a style of speaking that was the best fit for who I was as a communicator and that would best advance the vision of our church. I chose to focus on topical preaching with one primary point in every weekend message. I began to do messages in series so that the overall theme of the series would serve to make every message more memorable. This approach was consistent with our goal of changed lives.

Elevating my weekend messages became my highest priority.

In their book *Communicating for a Change*, Andy Stanley and Lane Jones encourage the adoption of a communication style that results in application not just contemplation. Andy writes,

> [My goal] is to teach people how to live a life that reflects the values, principles and truths of the Bible. In short, my goal is change. I want them to do something different instead of just think about it. When I'm finished preaching, I want people in the audience to know what to do with what they have heard. And I want them to walk away motivated to give it a try.[5]

If you are a pastor, it may seem impossible to be able to invest the time and energy needed to make every weekend message clear and compelling enough to result in genuine life change. But you have to find a way. If not, your messages will never be close to what they could be and neither will your church. Elevate your messages. You owe it to the people you are called to reach, including the next generation.

MONEY ISSUES

The commitment to become a new generation church is a very costly commitment. It is costly, of course, in terms of the internal and external conflicts that arise from the change, but it also costs a lot of money.

Some of the changes will result in a savings. For example, every program and ministry that is eliminated will no longer need to be funded. But you definitely will not be spending less money! Staffing costs will almost certainly increase. Some of your goals may be accomplished by reassigning current staff members to responsibilities that better match the new focus of the church. But most likely you will find that you need some additional full-time or part-time staff members to lead a dynamic children's and youth ministry or to provide youthful worship leadership during weekend services.

Costs will also increase due to investments needed in other areas you have identified as essential to fulfilling your vision. The biggest new expense by far for Amplify Church was related to facility changes in our attempt to create "irresistible environments" for children and young adults. We spent an average of 10 percent of the annual church budget on expenses directly related to reaching the next generation—primarily on facility transformation. One year we spent close to 20 percent. This was a tremendous step of faith for our board of directors, but we were convinced that the things we were investing in would have a major impact on our ability to reach children and youth and their parents.

I recently found a note I had written before returning to full-time ministry that read, "Money won't be a problem." It was a statement of faith. Then we started our turnaround, and reality set in. It *felt* to me like money was *always* a problem. For years, the total in our bank account was close to the amount of the previous weekend's offering. But we somehow found a way to make it work.

We made giving easier by providing online giving and other options like kiosks, smartphone apps, and giving via text message. I knew we had to provide those options when a number of new members in their twenties indicated that they did not have a checkbook. But it wasn't about creative giving options or ingenious fund-raising. When all was said and done, people gave generously because they believed in the vision of the church. I guess that the statement "Money won't be a problem" has turned out to be true, because a lack of money hasn't stopped us from doing what we felt God was calling us to do.

By the way, I know that some churches that have few or no children and youth coming on the weekend have a significant amount of money in the bank. If this describes your church, start investing in the next generation! A pastor from another church once walked through our children's and youth environments and said, "I wish we had the money sitting around to do this, because our church is dying and we really need to reach young people." I let him know that even though our church budget had grown, we still had the same amount of money "sitting around" as when we started—almost nothing. We were spending whatever we had to build a new generation church. To my shock, he mentioned that his church had over a million dollars in the bank. They didn't want to touch it, though, because the church was in decline and they might need the money for a rainy day. I felt no sympathy for their situation. None whatsoever.

VOLUNTEERISM

At Amplify Church we did not have the money to hire enough staff members to do what was needed to become a new generation church. Just hiring one new staff person at a modest salary was a huge stretch for our budget. In fact, no matter how much we grew, we knew we could never hire enough paid staff to do what must be done to remain a new generation church. So we had to become a volunteer-driven church.

Volunteerism was not a new concept. Our church already had many good people who volunteered their time. But we needed a much larger percentage of those who attended our church to volunteer in some capacity. We also needed those who currently volunteered, especially with children and youth and the new music ministry, to spend more time in preparation.

All of this seemed impossible, of course. How could we increase our volunteer numbers and ask for more commitment, all while some people were leaving the church because of the changes and others were in a "wait and see" mode? Yet somehow it happened. People who were already attending the church jumped in because they were energized by the renewed vision for outreach and growth. They were joined by new attendees who started to volunteer when they saw how much there was to do.

Before long we had small group leaders and children's and youth workers and worship team members who spent a significant amount of time preparing for their roles. We had members who hadn't volunteered for anything in the past helping out as parking lot attendants, greeters, café workers, and in other roles. Volunteerism became contagious.

"I DON'T EVEN RECOGNIZE MY OWN CHURCH!"

I know that some changes we made to elevate our standards might seem inappropriate, especially if those changes threatened long-held church traditions. We concluded that we would find little comfort in preserving traditions if we were not reaching people. Leaders and members of every type of church who are serious about getting and staying connected to the next generation must be willing to make significant changes, including elevating the weekend services, elevating the music, and elevating the messages.

> No matter what type of church you attend, you will find little comfort in preserving traditions if you are not reaching people.

Truth be told, I would not want to live through the first two years of our church's changes again. We implemented rapid, sweeping change. We did not just paint our Vega silver. But I knew we were making progress in elevating our standards when a common reason people gave for inviting others was because we always did things at our church with excellence. We still have a long way to go, but we definitely have started to close the gap between where we were and where we could be.

I find it fascinating that some of those who initially were the most skeptical of our dramatic changes ended up being the biggest supporters. One woman stands out to me: Eleanor Evans. I recently conducted her funeral when she died at age ninety-five. Eleanor had attended the church for almost thirty years. She was in her mideighties when the church started to change, but she didn't leave like many of her friends. She stayed. She prayed that the changes would make a real difference in our ability to reach the next generation. She even started to give special offerings toward the transformation of the children's areas.

After a few years, I had one of my many conversations with Eleanor. I assumed that she had warmed up to the changes we made to the adult service. I asked her if the new style of music had grown on her. She said, "No. I don't really care for the new music. I wear earplugs because it is loud." I was somewhat taken aback, and I asked her, "Why do you keep coming and praying and giving?" She said, "Because now my children and my grandchildren will come to church with me. And I look around every week at the children and grandchildren of others who are filling our church. That means everything to me."

People like Eleanor are the heroes of our change. She may not have been young, but she was certainly young at heart. She came to love the energy that young people brought to our church. She drew great satisfaction from seeing her church filled with people of all ages. She looked past the youthful dress and tattoos of many of the new attendees, seeing people who could know Christ as intimately as she knew him. She helped to make that happen with her prayers, support, and giving.

I remember one Sunday morning right before the service started when Eleanor called me over to her seat on the end of the third row in the middle aisle. She pointed out to me the people of all ages who were pouring into our sanctuary. She exclaimed, "I don't even recognize my own church!" Her words were not spoken in anger or dismay. Her words were spoken in wonder and gratitude at God's amazing work.

APPLICATION

Silver Vega

Readings

Start children off on the way they should go, and even when they are old they will not turn from it.

Proverbs 22:6

People were bringing little children to Jesus for him to place his hands on them, but the disciples rebuked them. When Jesus saw this, he was indignant. He said to them, "Let the little children come to me, and do not hinder them, for the kingdom of God belongs to such as these. Truly I tell you, anyone who will not receive the kingdom of God like a little child will never enter it." And he took the children in his arms, placed his hands on them and blessed them.

Mark 10:13–16

APPLICATION

Silver Vega

Discussion Questions

1. Do you think that modest changes in your church's approach will be sufficient to reach the next generation or will it take significant change? Why?

2. Do you think that your church's weekend services (including the musical style and excellence) have a positive, neutral, or negative effect on your church's ability to reach the next generation?

3. What is the current "level of courage" in your church for the kind of changes that you think it will take to reach the next generation? What is your personal level of courage?

4. If your church commits to becoming a new generation church, would you be willing (and able) to increase the amount of time and energy you invest as a volunteer? Share the reasons for your answers if you are comfortable doing so.

5. If your church commits to becoming a new generation church, would your personal financial giving to your church most likely increase, decrease, or stay the same? Share the reasons for your answers if you are comfortable doing so.

APPLICATION
Silver Vega

Action Planning

Strategy #4: Elevate Your Standards

List significant ways that you could elevate your standards as a church that would better fulfill your church's vision and reach the next generation. Make sure to include ways to elevate the weekend worship experience for adults and children.

Prayer

Father God, I come to you in Jesus' name. Help me (us) to be open to the significant changes that we should make in our church and the right timing and pace of those changes.

CHAPTER 5

DON'T BE LIKE JOSHUA

More than three thousand years ago, Joshua led Israel to great victories and into a time of peace, stability, and spiritual vitality. Under Joshua's leadership, the nation thrived, accomplishing God's purposes for that generation. We don't have insight into exactly what Joshua and his generation did or didn't do to have an impact on the faith of their children and grandchildren, but we do know the end result was horrifying.

> After a while the people of Joshua's generation died, and the next generation did not know the Lord or any of the things he had done for Israel. The Lord had brought their ancestors out of Egypt, and they had worshiped him. But now the Israelites stopped worshiping the Lord and worshiped the idols of Baal and Astarte, as well as the idols of other gods from nearby nations.
>
> The Lord was so angry.
>
> *Judges 2:10–13 CEV*

We cannot control what will happen to the next generation when we are gone, but we can do everything possible to pave the way for them. When King David realized that the temple would not be built during his lifetime, he set up his son Solomon for success. He made the key arrangements for the construction project, including securing an extensive list of materials he knew Solomon would need.

Like David, most of us do our best to set up our children and grandchildren for success in practical areas such as finances. We must also pave the way spiritually. Building a church that truly engages the next generation is a part of our legacy as parents and as leaders. In the book *The 21 Irrefutable Laws of Leadership*, John Maxwell writes:

> Just about anybody can make an organization look good for a moment—by launching a flashy new program or product, drawing crowds to a big event, or slashing the budget to boost the bottom line. But leaders who leave a legacy take a different approach. They lead with tomorrow as well as today in mind. . . . When all is said and done, your ability as a leader will not be judged by what you achieved personally or even by what your team accomplished during your tenure. You will be judged by how well your people and your organization did after you were gone.[1]

My daughter and her husband have lived in Brooklyn, New York, for several years and help to oversee Connect Groups (small groups) at Hillsong New York. I marvel each time I attend church with them at the line of young adults that wraps around the block as they wait to get inside. It certainly challenges the notion that young people don't want to go to church anymore! Hillsong New York reflects the passion and vision of Hillsong Church founder Brian Houston, who writes in his book *For This I Was Born: Aligning Your Vision to God's Cause*:

> We are all on loan to this world, and while here, we are simply stewards of the vision God has given us. One day a new generation will take over where we leave off, and I pray they will pursue with even greater fervor the things of God. . . . We all need to be committed to empowering future generations to do even greater exploits in God's name than we have done and to believe that the Lord will give them vision for things we could never imagine. I believe we have a responsibility to the legend and legacy we will leave to those who come after us. Put simply, your vision is not just for you; it is for those to come.[2]

STRATEGY #5: BUILD A MENTORING CULTURE

If we want to set up the next generation for success, we must build a mentoring culture in our churches. This is why I think of church revitalization as more than just turning around a church in decline, which may lead to a season of temporary revitalization. I believe we need to think in terms of *perpetual* church revitalization—*putting appropriate strategies in place to ensure that a church will connect with and stay connected with the next generation.* For most leaders, it seems hard enough just to build a new generation church, but we must also put into place the practices required to make sure our church stays a new generation church.

Paving the way for the next generation is not just something for church leaders close to retirement to consider. Unexpected things can happen. Consider your own church: if one or more senior leaders in your church were immediately gone for whatever reason, would your church be prepared to continue to effectively fulfill its God-given vision?

The bottom line is that your church will likely fail to become and remain a vibrant force in your community without embracing *and* institutionalizing new-generation-church thinking. Therefore you will need to put into place practices and policies like the following, which are designed to keep new-generation-church thinking an ongoing part of a church's DNA.

THREE-DEEP MENTORING

Every leader at Amplify Church commits to mentor at least two people who can effectively carry out each of their key roles. That allows us to be "three-deep" (the leader plus the two people being mentored) at every key role in the church. Leaders are told constantly that their leadership effectiveness is best demonstrated when they are not present. Being told, "I am so glad you are back from vacation; it went badly without you here," is not seen by a leader as a compliment. Rather, it is an indictment of their poor leadership skills. Our full-time staff members are required to identify those they are mentoring for each area they lead as part of their written performance plan.

Three-deep mentoring starts with the primary communicators who do weekend messages. We do our messages in series so that whoever is speaking takes the topic that fits into the series at that time. When I am not speaking, I typically assign the weekend message to one of the young communicators I am mentoring. I spend time coaching that person for success and making sure they are given both positive feedback and feedback for improvement. Our church has become accustomed to young leaders in the church speaking during weekend services even when I am not away. Their speaking sends a strong message about preparing the next generation to lead.

> Being told, "I am so glad you are back from vacation; it went badly without you here," is not seen as a compliment. Rather, it is an indictment of their poor leadership skills.

One unexpected development occurred after our church started growing again. Due to requests from people who were traveling relatively long distances to get to our church, we began to replicate our weekend services in "extension campuses" within a one-hour drive of our main campus. Rather than make these extension campuses video-based by showing a video message from our main campus, we schedule a live communicator for each extension campus service. This helps to ensure that we have regular opportunities for our young communicators to grow and develop.

The three-deep principle applies to other areas in the church as well, including worship leaders, our tech team, children's and youth ministry leaders, small group leaders, and so on. All leaders are commonly asked, "Who are the people you are mentoring who can step in when you are not here?" Instead of waiting for an opportunity to serve until the mentor is sick or on vacation, those being mentored are regularly rotated into the schedule. Those who are being mentored are usually younger than the mentors, which reinforces our commitment to prepare the next generation.

SUCCESSION PLANNING

Every church that is serious about being a new generation church must take seriously succession planning for the role of senior pastor. In their book *Next: Pastoral Succession That Works*, William Vanderbloemen and Warren Bird argue that while there is no single scriptural template, succession planning must be a priority in every church:

> Sooner or later, unless Jesus returns during your lifetime, there will be a pastoral transition. Thinking about that transition ahead of time might make all the difference in your and your church's legacy. . . .
>
> [Creating a succession plan] is something any pastor or leadership team in any church can do at some level—regardless of age, church size, or denomination/tradition.[3]

Your church may belong to a denomination or tradition that already has a process for replacing your senior pastor in the event of a vacancy. If that is the case, do everything possible to influence the process so that it does not compromise your commitment to be a new generation church. A process that results in an interim pastor serving for an extended period of time who does not understand or support reaching the next generation can stall your church's momentum. A succession process that results in a new senior pastor, no matter what his or her age, who is not committed to a new-generation-church approach would be devastating.

> **Every church that is serious about being a new generation church must take seriously succession planning for the role of senior pastor.**

For nondenominational churches like Amplify Church, effective succession planning may be even more critical. In the event of a vacancy in the role of senior pastor, our original church bylaws called for the organization of a search committee, followed by several candidates speaking at the church, and culminating in a congregational vote. This occurred three times in our church history, and every time the process resulted in major destabilization in the church. In every transition, a large percentage of the people who voted no for the incoming senior pastor left the church. Although it seems to be democratic, the idea of congregational voting for the selection of a pastor is not mandated or even found in the Scriptures. In our church, that approach led to division and discord.

Since Scripture gives little guidance regarding church government and structure, these things should be shaped or reshaped to best ensure that the church becomes and remains a new generation church. Thankfully, we had already changed our bylaws to combine the boards of our church. Prior to these transitions, we had been operating with a board of elders, responsible for spiritual matters, and a board of directors, responsible for practical matters. Unfortunately, these boards were often in conflict with one another over who had the authority to do what since so many topics in the church were both spiritual and practical. Much time and energy was wasted in these discussions. We now have one board of directors made up of spiritual people who oversee the financial and legal issues of the church. The staff, with the help of small group leaders and other volunteers, oversee the day-to-day practical operations of the church.

When it came to succession planning, we revised the Amplify Church bylaws to make it the responsibility of the senior pastor to nominate a successor to the board of directors. Assuming the person nominated is approved, it becomes the responsibility of the senior pastor to mentor that person to be ready to step in when needed. Whether the senior pastor is suddenly gone for unexpected reasons or a transition is several years away, the successor has been identified and a quick and orderly transition can take place. Most important, the new senior pastor will have already embraced and been practicing the principles required to lead a new generation church.

We take this very seriously. For example, I have a policy that I don't fly on the same plane as my successor. We don't often drive in the same car, especially on a lengthy trip. While it is sometimes inconvenient and may seem overly cautious, both of us are highly committed to the future of the church. We know that many people have given and sacrificed to make the church healthy again, and we are willing to put up with some small inconveniences to try to ensure that the future of the church is secure.

While succession planning for the senior pastor role is

of utmost importance, we also practice succession planning in other key roles. For instance, lead pastors of our extension campuses are asked to identify and mentor a successor as well. In conjunction with the principles behind "three-deep mentoring," successors are also identified and developed for key roles such as worship director, youth director, and children's director.

THE 75 PERCENT RULE

I have found that people in their fifties, sixties, and older tend to be very open to attending a church where the majority of people in visible leadership are significantly younger than they are. On the other hand, I have found that it is less likely that young adults and young parents will be drawn to a weekend service where the vast majority of people in visible leadership are significantly older than they are.

That is why we instituted the *75 percent rule*. The 75 percent rule is that *75 percent of all of the people in visible leadership during any given weekend service must be the average age of or younger than the community we serve.* For Amplify Church, that means that 75 percent of those in visible leadership during any given weekend service need to be thirty-five years old or younger. That requires us to identify a lot of young people who can speak effectively, lead worship, play instruments, and do the announcements!

Think about your church services over the past few months. If a high percentage of the people who were up front—those who spoke, did readings, shared announcements, led singing, and played instruments—were older than the average age of the community you serve, chances are your services are less appealing to young people than you may realize.

I remember a comment made by a woman in her early twenties who visited our church. She came reluctantly in response to an invitation from a friend. After her first service, she told me, "I'll definitely be coming back." I asked her why, and she said, "Because so many of the people up front look like me." Even if you use 50 percent as your goal instead of 75 percent (as we did when we started our turnaround), you will at least be committed to having young people involved every weekend in visible leadership.

When I was a young pastor, I visited a church that I admired for their excellence in ministry. The people who were in visible leadership in teaching and music and other key areas of ministry were also, for the most part, in their thirties. I marveled at their teamwork and effectiveness. The church was filled with people of all ages, and the energy was palpable.

The 75 percent rule is that 75 percent of all of the people in visible leadership during any given weekend service must be the average age of or younger than the community we serve.

Twenty years later, I visited that church again. The same people were teaching. The same people were leading worship. They were just twenty years older. The congregation seemed to be about twenty years older too. It's easy for this to happen unless there is a deep commitment to purposefully mentor the next generation and open the door for their talents to be used.

We do whatever it takes to get young adults ready for visible leadership. Since I was a guitar teacher during my high school and college years, there was a period of time when I wrote out the guitar leads in music tablature for our young guitarists. I didn't have the extra time to do this, but I believed that mentoring others was critical, and mentoring was becoming a way of life for our church. Seeing those teenagers and young adults, when musically proficient, playing during adult weekend services was deeply rewarding. Embracing the 75 percent rule requires a determination to proactively prepare young adults to lead and then to give them the chance to lead.

Embracing the 75 percent rule requires a determination to proactively prepare young adults to lead and then give them the chance to lead.

I am not saying that people over thirty-five years old do not have significant leadership roles in our church. In fact, the roles filled by our members in their forties, fifties, sixties, and older provide the strong and stable foundation without which we could not be a strong and stable church. In addition to the natural mentoring they do with our young leaders, they fill many of our most critical leadership roles, from children's and youth ministry to pastoral care. People over thirty-five years old currently make up our entire board of directors. They also make up a very high percentage of our small group leaders, perhaps the most critical role in the church.

One of our church members who makes a significant "behind the scenes" contribution is a woman in her sixties who has served as a volunteer continuously for more than thirty years. For many years, she created the overhead transparencies that were used for our worship services. Later she adapted to creating PowerPoint slides on a PC. Now she prepares the entire service using ProPresenter on a Mac. With constant changes in technology, she was pushed further and further out of her comfort zone, but to her credit, she adapted. She serves from a booth in our balcony and knows that she is making a tremendous contribution even though she is not in a visible up-front role.

The 75 percent rule does require that talented people at Amplify Church in their forties and fifties and older be willing to step aside from being up front every week during weekend services—even when people in the church are telling them how much they are missed when they don't play or sing or speak. I admire them greatly because they have embraced our vision for mentoring younger leaders and have stepped up to the challenge. They know that by letting go of their "right" to be up front every week, they are opening the door for the next generation.

In some ways, placing older people in visible leadership roles is easier, since giving young leaders a platform comes with risks. One of our worship leaders in his twenties became visibly intoxicated at a wedding reception where other church members were present. Another worship team singer became pregnant while unmarried. Both were quietly removed from their roles for a season. When you are committed to putting young adults into visible leadership roles, you certainly will have to deal with very different issues than you would deal with if all of those in visible leadership roles were over forty.

That said, giving young people visible leadership roles is worth the challenges involved. And it isn't just about making the church feel young. It is a necessary aspect of effectively relating to the next generation. Researcher David Kinnaman writes:

Today the influences of technology, pop culture, media, entertainment, science, and an increasingly secular society are intensifying the differences between the generations. And many churches, leaders, and parents—the established generation—have a difficult time understanding these differences, much less relating to the values, beliefs, and assumptions that have spawned them. So we need younger leaders. . . . Young leaders who speak the language of their peers are sorely needed because today's twentysomethings are not just slightly or incrementally different from previous generations.[4]

THE AMPLIFY LEADERSHIP DEVELOPMENT SYSTEM

In conjunction with a cohort of churches pulled together by the Leadership Network, Amplify Church developed a leadership development system to reinforce our commitment to build a mentoring culture. The goal of this system is to create an ongoing "pipeline" of leaders so that the vision of the church will never be compromised due to a lack of ready leaders.

We start with the premise that everyone we need to be a leader is currently a part of our church. With the exception of the music and youth director who was hired in 2003, every staff member has been hired from within Amplify Church. Sometimes hiring from outside of the church is the right thing to do, and there are some great search firms and denominational leaders who can help connect you with the right person. But I would suggest that you begin by looking within and resist the natural tendency to overlook an internal candidate who has high potential in order to bring in the "perfect" candidate from outside of your church. Someone from the outside may seem to be an excellent fit because of their resume and skill set, but you have not lived with their inevitable quirks and weaknesses as you have with those inside your church. Most important, it is very difficult to know how they will resonate in the long run with the vision and leadership of the church.

Our approach to staffing is that we recruit volunteers from those who are attending the church by "shoulder-tapping," or personally inviting, a person to step into a particular volunteer role that seems to be a possible good fit for that person. We have found this to be far more effective than just making general appeals during weekend services. For a few of those volunteers, we create internships so they can engage in-depth in some area of ministry. We recruit part-time staff members from our volunteers or interns. We recruit full-time staff members from our part-time staff members. If they require a seminary education or other specific training for their role, we often help them financially to get the continuing education they need.

We start with the premise that everyone we need to be a leader is currently a part of our church.

The benefits of this approach are significant. We never have a question about the individual's passion for the vision of the church. They have already bought into our vision. We never have a question about the individual's respect for those in church leadership. They have already been following the lead of those in positions of authority in the church. We never have a question about the individual's sincerity and faithfulness because we have already observed it firsthand.

Our leadership development system prepares people for the five most common leadership roles in which people serve at Amplify Church:

- volunteer team or small group assistant leader
- volunteer team or small group leader
- assistant ministry director
- ministry director
- campus lead pastor

We expect every leader in every role to embrace our vision and model our core values. In addition, each leadership role has specific attributes that we look for and develop. Since each role has progressively more responsibility, the corresponding attributes are more challenging. When a person is being mentored for a future role, the leadership attributes related to that future role become the focal point of their development.

AMPLIFY CHURCH LEADERSHIP ROLE	LEADERSHIP ATTRIBUTES		
Campus Lead Pastor	Visionary	Courageous	Culture Builder
Ministry Director	Big-Picture Focus	Decisive	Team Builder
Assistant Ministry Director	Goal Driven	Loyal	Empowering
Volunteer Team/ Small Group Leader	Proactive	Trustworthy	Influential
Volunteer Team/ Small Group Assistant Leader	Dependable	Teachable	Caring

To develop leaders church-wide with similar skill sets, we adjusted our roles and our organizational chart to create as much consistency as possible across all of our campuses. This allows for people to move relatively seamlessly from one campus to another as needed. We also developed a coaching guide to give our leaders a better idea of how to develop those whom they are mentoring in the attributes they need for future success.

Leaders who do not reflect our values or the targeted leadership attributes for their role are given feedback and, if necessary, moved to other roles in the church. We also purposefully expand the level of empowerment we give to volunteers as they progress to roles with wider responsibilities. Even though I exercised a "leader-driven" approach during the first couple of years of our church's turnaround, we are firm believers that the default leadership style in our church should be a high-involvement, empowering leadership style.

DIVERSITY AND MULTICULTURALISM

While we often see differences between generations as problems to overcome, there is value in highlighting the strengths that younger generations have in effective ministry. One of the many ways that young leaders in today's culture positively influence the church is in their approach to diversity and multiculturalism.

I recently spoke at a church in Northern California that was created as a merger of two churches, an aging Caucasian church and a Filipino church. The older members of both churches had a deep commitment to Christ-inspired diversity.

Each church accommodated the preferences of the other. Half of the music consisted of traditional hymns accompanied by an organ in the style preferred by the Caucasian church. The other half of the music consisted of choruses led by a worship band made up of people from the Filipino church. The pastors of both churches took turns doing the weekend messages. Their unity was a remarkable testimony, and I was encouraged to see them working so hard to honor one another. Yet despite their commitment to unity and their desire to work together, the church still had the feel of two separate congregations meeting in one building. I suspect that most visitors would share my impressions, feeling as if they were attending two churches at once.

Over the years, I have attended many diversity conferences and workshops that have encouraged diversity and multiculturalism in the workplace or in the church. My generation, the baby boomer generation, has worked hard to embrace diversity and multiculturalism because we know it is the wise and right thing to do. That is why I found it strange never to hear our young leaders talking about the topic. I have learned that they don't talk about it; they just live it. They seem to be much more inclined to naturally appreciate racial and cultural distinctions. As a result, our church has naturally become more diverse as we have put young adults into visible leadership roles. Each of our campuses pretty closely reflects the community in which it exists in both age and diversity.

I cannot imagine the challenges faced by declining churches in a community with demographics that are in stark contrast to the demographics of the church. That was not our situation.

The solutions for churches in that situation are complex, to say the least. But I propose that part of the solution for any church committed to diversity and multiculturalism is putting the next generation in visible leadership roles in the church.

"ALMOST NO ONE COMES TO CHURCH HERE ANYMORE"

During a visit to a breathtaking cathedral in Germany, I asked the guide how many people worshiped there each weekend. His answer was heartbreaking: "Almost no one comes to church here anymore—just tourists and a few elderly people." Thinking of our churches as being potentially one generation away from extinction is not being overly dramatic. Someone has said that we are either living out the birth of a new vision or the death of an old one. The members of every church must decide which it will be.

We are either living out the birth of a new vision or the death of an old one. The members of every church must decide which it will be.

Joshua and his peers lived rich and full lives marked by God's presence and power. I suspect that during their lives they felt that things were fine. You may feel that way about your church right now. But somehow Joshua and his peers failed to engage the next generation in a meaningful way. Their children, the next generation, did not know the Lord. Don't make the same mistake. Don't be like Joshua.

IT WAS WORTH THE FIGHT

Building a new generation church at Amplify was tedious and trying, especially in the first two years. Many times I found myself asking, "Why are we doing this?" I know now that it was worth the fight.

- It was worth the fight for a new generation of young people who are far from God and need to hear the message of Christ in a way that profoundly connects with them.
- It was worth the fight for a new generation of older people who are far from God and have never experienced a church that makes the timeless truths of the Scriptures relevant to their lives.
- It was worth the fight for a new generation of Christ followers who experience a deeper relationship with God by caring more about reaching others than holding on to personal preferences.

We easily could have avoided the hard work that has gone into the strategies we implemented to become a new generation church, including building a mentoring culture. Our church probably could have survived as it was, designed around our personal preferences, at least for several more years. All we had to do was let other churches worry about reaching the next generation. But we decided that it was worth the hard work. We decided that it was worth the fight. How about you?

APPLICATION

Don't Be Like Joshua

Readings

Only be careful, and watch yourselves closely so that you do not forget the things your eyes have seen or let them fade from your heart as long as you live. Teach them to your children and to their children after them.

Deuteronomy 4:9

But you must remain faithful to the things you have been taught. You know they are true, for you know you can trust those who taught you.

2 Timothy 3:14 NLT

APPLICATION
Don't Be Like Joshua

Discussion Questions

1. What do you think our responsibility is when it comes to paving the way for the next generation?

2. How would you describe the mentoring of young people that is happening intentionally in your church?

3. How supportive would you be if your church opened the door proactively for young people to have visible positions of leadership during weekend services?

4. What can you do personally to make sure that your church becomes and remains a new generation church?

APPLICATION

Don't Be Like Joshua

Action Planning

Strategy #5: Build a Mentoring Culture

List practices or systems that should be put in place to ensure that your church becomes and remains a new generation church.

Prayer

Father God, I come to you in Jesus' name. Help me (us) to have the courage not just to discuss what we should do to reach the next generation but to find a way to do it.

CONCLUSION

Many years ago I was asked to perform a funeral for a man I had never met. I met with several family members to learn about his life so I could personalize the service. I asked, "What is it that you will remember most about him?" There was dead silence. I prompted them again with the same question. More silence.

Finally, a response came: "He drank a lot of ice water. He always seemed to have a glass of ice water in his hand." Everyone nodded in agreement, so I wrote that down and asked, "What else?" There was another long, uncomfortable silence until someone else finally spoke up and said, "He sure liked his ice water." I remember thinking at the time that I did not want to leave an ice-water legacy.

I was talking to a pastor not long ago who was convinced that he would only answer to God about how he and the people of his church used their gifts during his lifetime. He said, "What happens after I am gone is up to God." As you would expect, he had done little to prepare the church for the future.

If we are held accountable for using our gifts to make a difference in this world during our time on earth, doesn't it make sense that we are also accountable as leaders to unearth and develop the gifts of the next generation? I think it does.

I don't want our church to be alive for our generation only to become extinct once the current church members are gone. That would be an ice-water legacy.

You can build a church that will make a difference in this world for generations to come. You can build a church that reaches the hearts of and unearths the gifts of your children and grandchildren and great-grandchildren.

NEXT STEPS

If you decide to take action, I suggest using the strategies outlined in this book as a framework for determining the practical actions that are right for your church. The questions at the end of each chapter related to each strategy should be helpful in reaching consensus about the changes that are appropriate for your church.

Consider working through those questions with your guiding coalition, the small group of staff members or church members who can help to think through what it will take to mobilize the church as a whole to become a new generation church. A one- or two-day retreat for your guiding coalition/leadership team, with or without an external facilitator, could be a great way to jump-start the process.

The chart in the appendix of this book lists practical actions that we took at Amplify Church for each of the five strategies and the timing for each. You will note that just about every action listed was taken during the first two years of our change journey. I recommend that you adopt a two-year time frame for implementing your primary changes.

In review, the five strategies that you need to address follow:

#1: Adopt a New Mindset. Do whatever is needed to shift the mindset of the people of your church away from the statement "If it was good enough for me, it is good enough for our children," and replace it with the question "What will it take to reach and continue to reach the next generation?"

#2: Identify the Essentials. Clarify the vision that you believe God wants for your church and then identify your "vision essentials"—the handful of things that deserve your time, attention, energy, and resources because they are absolutely essential to achieving your vision.

#3: Reduce the Distractions. Identify and eliminate as many church programs, ministries, and practices as possible that potentially distract members and visitors from your vision. Redirect your time, attention, energy, and resources to the things that are essential to fulfilling your vision.

#4: Elevate Your Standards. Pursue excellence by closing the gap between where you are as a church and where you have the potential to be, including elevating your weekend services, music, and messages.

#5: Build a Mentoring Culture. Put into place practices and systems that ensure that the next generation is prepared for and placed into visible leadership roles in the church, and also ensure that the church will become and remain a new generation church.

Though this book revolves around these strategies and the related actions that you may take, nothing of consequence happens without prayer. As the psalmist wrote, "Unless the Lord builds the house, the builders labor in vain" (Psalm 127:1).

Pray for wisdom. Pray for courage. Pray for favor. Most of all, acknowledge in prayer your dependence on God to bring genuine church transformation. Only God can open the hearts of the people who are in your church. Only God can open the hearts of the people you are trying to reach, including your children and grandchildren.

WHATEVER IT TAKES

I don't know what it will take for your church to become and remain a new generation church. The changes that we made at Amplify Church put us on the right track. For many older members in the church, there were too many changes. But for many of the hundreds of young adults, young parents, and children who now attend Amplify Church, the course of their lives has been changed forever. Many of our new attendees had not been attending church anywhere. They come to Amplify Church because it is a place where they and their families can make a meaningful connection with God.

I hope that the list of changes we made provokes you to a prayerful willingness to do whatever it takes. Your list of necessary changes will likely be very different. Just remember, making such changes will not threaten your core beliefs and mission but instead will help to preserve them. Accepting the status quo is the greatest threat to your church's core mission and, perhaps, to the very survival of your church.

> Accepting the status quo is the greatest threat to your church's core mission and, perhaps, to the very survival of your church.

I hope that when my days on earth are over that it is said of me, "He paved the way for generations to come." I hope that it is said of the people of our church, "They paved the way for generations to come." My hope is that the same will be said of you.

AFTERWORD

When our family first moved to Atlanta in 1997, we transformed the lower level of our home into a place that our high school–aged daughters and their friends would want to spend a lot of time. We bought a pool table and a pinball machine, and we installed a state-of-the-art home theater. Our hopes were realized. Even though our daughters were the "new kids in town," their friends would hang out at our house several nights a week.

I remember spending several months searching for the right coffee table to put in front of the leather sectional sofa in the home theater. I finally found the ideal table—crafted of black marble in Italy. It was far too expensive, but it was the final perfect piece to complete our home theater.

One month after the marble table arrived and I put it in our home theater room, I came home to find that it had been broken into two pieces and could not be repaired. The high school students who were invited guests in our home had destroyed it.

When I learned that my daughter's friends had broken our perfect marble table in half, I was furious. Then I gave it some thought and philosophically arrived at what I call the "Marble Table Principle": *The only way to avoid the troubles and challenges related to children and young adults is if they are not around.* If we did not have all of those teenagers hanging out at our home, my marble table would still be intact. But that was not a trade I was willing to make.

GET READY FOR TROUBLE

Let's assume that you actually pull off what it takes to transform your church into a new generation church and your church starts to be filled with children and young adults. Get ready. You will soon face challenges and troubles that aging congregations seldom face.

First, you need to take a fresh look at the security of your church, especially as it relates to children's ministry. Parents need to know that you are as serious as they are when it comes to the safety of their children. In addition to background checks on every person who works with your children and youth, you need to create a rigorous check-in and pick-up process for the children who come to church each weekend. We have chosen to pay an officer from the local police force to be in our building and to be highly visible for every weekend service. Our bottom-line message to parents is that we will seek to create a safe and nurturing environment in which their children can develop a growing relationship with Jesus Christ.

At Amplify Church we have a "two-person" policy that no staff

Our bottom-line message to parents is that we will seek to create a safe and nurturing environment in which their children can develop a growing relationship with Jesus Christ.

person or volunteer can be alone at any time with a child or young adult who is under eighteen or has not graduated from high school. This makes life more difficult for youth leaders who are committed to discipleship and know the power of one-on-one mentoring in building relationships with teens. Yet despite the added hassles, this policy provides a safety net for both young people and youth workers.

We have also adopted a controversial philosophy at Amplify Church that guides our decision making and is especially important in times of crisis. As church leaders, we firmly believe in both child safety and the life-changing power of Jesus Christ. *We have chosen to prioritize our commitment to child safety over our belief that people can genuinely change.* We did not embrace this philosophy quickly or easily. We adopted it only after a contentious debate that dominated several meetings of the board of directors over many months. The reason this was such a difficult discussion is because we have seen countless lives genuinely change through faith in Christ.

For instance, if we become aware of a person who attends the church who is a convicted or confessed child molester, we ask them to sign an agreement that they will be present only in our foyer and sanctuary and only during weekend services. If they do not sign the agreement or are found to be in violation of the agreement, they disqualify themselves from any involvement at Amplify Church. One person in that situation angrily left the church, declaring that he did not want to be a part of a church with leaders who did not trust that he had changed. I fully understood his point of view, but we chose not to risk the safety of our children on the hope that he was a changed man.

This philosophy was key to our decision-making process when a part-time youth staff member faced criminal charges regarding a seventeen-year-old girl from our youth group. This staff member had passed all of the required background checks, was employed full-time by a local high school, and had served for years as a volunteer without incident. As a result of these charges, the board of directors decided that he would no longer be permitted on church property or to attend church activities. We prioritized child safety. Though you may choose to handle a similar situation in a different way, it is wise to have policies in place that will serve to guide your decision making.

WHEN CRISIS COMES

I hope that you never face such a child-related crisis, but if you do, let me suggest three things:

1. Act quickly and decisively. Decisions made by church leadership often are painfully slow and take far longer than necessary. Debates by various boards and committees can keep the church in a prolonged state of paralysis. In a time of crisis, cutting through the bureaucracy and acting quickly is essential. Anything less will appear to the congregation and the community as being indecisive about the safety and well-being of your children. That perception is lethal to your goal of being a next generation church. It may even be interpreted as covering up the situation, which is often as damaging as the situation itself.

2. Communicate to the church with transparency and grace. Holding back information from the church during times of crisis and hoping that everything will blow over and people will be none the wiser may be tempting. But such an approach will compromise the trust that church leadership has spent years building with the congregation and community.

When I have anticipated the possibility of a church issue being covered by the news media or even being spread on social media, I have leaned toward making a statement to the church before people from our church hear about it through other channels. You need to use wisdom regarding how much to say, of course, but keeping trust with the people of the church is essential, and transparency used with wisdom is a trust builder.

One of the challenges we faced was with the state-licensed weekday child care center we sponsored for several years. One of the forty child care workers was accused of being too rough with children who were enrolled. I read this statement to the church during weekend services:

> One of our former child care workers has been accused of roughly or inappropriately handling children in her care. The first accusation that I became aware of was investigated by the state Office of Children, Youth and Families, and we were informed that the accusation was unfounded. When a second accusation came to our attention, the child care worker was immediately removed from her position.
>
> Let me assure you of this—we have been focused on one thing: to respond with the integrity and decisiveness that you should expect from the leadership of your church. We will stay relentlessly focused on our vision to

lead as many people—including children—as possible into a growing relationship with Jesus Christ.

One note about communicating with grace: although a crisis typically arises because people make poor or sinful choices, no one involved is an angel and no one involved is the devil. You must never forget that all of those involved are just people. You will have greater credibility when you resist the urge to name people, canonize people, or demonize people.

3. Learn what you can from the crisis and adjust policies accordingly. If a crisis does occur, review your current policies and procedures. Compare your policies with those of other churches that are filled with children and youth, and update them if necessary to make them at least equally rigorous. This is a wise course of action to take even before a crisis takes place. Make sure the policies you have in place are communicated clearly to your children's and youth workers, and ideally, have every children's and youth worker sign the policy statement. When all workers are aware of your policies, they will be more apt to avoid breaking those policies and will also have a heightened awareness if someone else is breaking them.

When the handful of children and young adults who were attending our church grew into dozens and then into hundreds, we were thrilled. We were somewhat naive not to anticipate that having a church filled with children and young adults could lead to significant difficulties and even crises—the kind of difficulties and crises that our aging, declining church never would have had to face had we stayed on our previous course.

I guess it all comes down to the Marble Table Principle:

The only way to avoid the troubles and challenges related to children and young adults is if they are not around. If we did not have all of those children and young adults attending our church, things would be much easier. But that is not a trade I am willing to make.

TWO-YEAR STRATEGY WORKSHEET FOR AMPLIFY CHURCH

STRATEGY #1: ADOPT A NEW MINDSET	TIMING/DATES
Guiding coalition of leaders goes on field trips to see and experience new generation churches.	Months 1–3
Guiding coalition of leaders reads books and articles about church revitalization and reaching the next generation.	Months 1–3
Focus multiple weekend messages on the need and reasons to shift the church's approach from keeping people to reaching people.	Months 1–6
Focus multiple weekend messages on the need and reasons to shift the mindset of people in the church from the statement "If it is good enough for me it is good enough for my children" to the question "What will it take to reach our children?"	Months 1–6
Initiate small group Bible studies about the importance of people and churches fulfilling their God-given purpose and vision. All members are encouraged to attend a small group, led primarily by members of the guiding coalition.	Months 3–12
Engage as many individuals as possible in face-to-face conversations with a goal of sparking passion for building a new generation church.	Year 1

STRATEGY #2: IDENTIFY THE ESSENTIALS	TIMING/DATES
Present a clear, concise, inspiring, and useful vision statement to the board of directors and congregation.	Months 1–3
Focus multiple weekend messages on the meaning of the newly adopted church vision—state the vision in every weekend service.	Month 1 and ongoing
Identify the "vision essentials" that are most critical in achieving our vision—the weekend service, small groups, and children's and youth ministry.	Months 1–3
Focus multiple weekend messages on the importance of directing our time, energy, and attention to the "vision essentials."	Month 1 and ongoing
End midweek services to increase time, energy, and attention on weekend services.	Month 1
End Sunday school and regular men's and women's ministry meetings to increase time, energy, and attention on small groups.	Months 3–6
Hire part-time youth director (also serves as music director).	Month 1
Invest in excellent children's and youth curriculum and train leaders and volunteers in how best to use the curriculum.	Month 3 and ongoing
Create new "irresistible" environments in which children and youth meet.	Month 3 and ongoing
Increase overall missions giving, but focus on a small number of organizations.	Month 3 and ongoing

STRATEGY #3: REDUCE THE DISTRACTIONS	TIMING/DATES
Cover dated church sign at main entrance with canvas sign created by local printer.	Month 1

Two-Year Strategy Worksheet for Amplify Church

Pave gravel and dirt parking lot.	After Year 2
Arrange for removal of radio tower from top of roof.	Months 1–3
Remove bulletin boards from church foyer and paint church foyer.	Months 1–6
Remove dated, used furniture from foyer area and sanctuary.	Months 1–3
Replace aging green pews and stained rust-colored chairs with modern individual seating.	After Year 2
End evangelism training program as competition to small groups.	Months 1–3
Relocate food bank to a church closer to food bank recipients to free up space for children's and youth programs.	Year 2
Relocate drug rehab program to another church to free up space for children's and youth programs.	Year 2
Close K–12 Christian school, freeing up space for children's and youth programs.	After Year 2
Remove special pastor's chair on platform and special parking places for staff.	Month 1
End formal dress code for weekend services.	Month 1
Move verbal prayer requests from weekend services to small groups.	Months 1–3
Stop political action activities, including distribution of voter guides.	Year 1
Eliminate "open microphone" and prayer lines and establish "Join in without standing out" policy for worshipers at weekend services.	Months 1–3
Change name of church to better reflect vision of church.	Month 1

STRATEGY #4: ELEVATE YOUR STANDARDS	TIMING/DATES
Update church website dramatically.	Year 1
Form creative team of staff and volunteers to plan how to increase the impact of weekend services.	Months 1–3
Add volunteer greeters.	Year 1
Add volunteer parking lot attendants.	Year 2
Create café off of foyer staffed by volunteers.	Year 2
Create "VIP Team" to greet first-time visitors.	After Year 2
Replace silence with upbeat contemporary worship music before and after weekend services.	Month 1
Reduce length of services from over ninety minutes to approximately sixty-five minutes, including a significant reduction in time devoted to announcements.	Month 1
Begin to use modern Bible translations (NIV, NLT, etc.) to make it easier for visitors to engage with the text.	Month 1
Move two crosses to adjacent walls in order to install video screens so words of worship songs and Bible passages can be projected.	Year 1
Change music style to Hillsong/Passion contemporary worship style.	Month 1
Hold auditions for worship team and significantly increase rehearsal time to increase excellence of music.	Month 1
Install audio, video, and lighting components in sanctuary to better match new style of worship music.	Year 2 and ongoing
Change color of sanctuary walls from white to darker colors to increase intimacy of weekend worship experience.	After Year 2
Begin to present one-point weekend messages in four- to six-week series to make them more memorable for listeners.	Month 1

STRATEGY #5: BUILD A MENTORING CULTURE	TIMING/DATES
Focus multiple weekend messages on the need and reasons to mentor the next generation to ensure the future viability of the church.	Year 1
Identify core leadership roles and the desired attributes for each role as part of Amplify Leadership Development System.	After Year 2
Institute a default policy of hiring from within people who have shown faithfulness as volunteers.	Year 1 and ongoing
Institute "three-deep mentoring" policy so that every church leader identifies two people they are mentoring for each of their key roles.	After Year 2
Change bylaws for succession-planning purposes.	Year 2
Appoint successor to senior pastor.	After Year 2
Institute 75 percent rule to increase number of young adults in visible leadership roles during weekend services.	After Year 2
Institute rigorous policies and procedures prioritizing the safety and well-being of children.	After Year 2
Expand target audience for mentoring to include various church leaders visiting Amplify Church for encouragement or inspiration.	After Year 2

NOTES

Introduction

1. George O. Wood, *My Mission*, http://georgeowood.com/about/my-mission/.
2. Tom Cheyney, *The Church Revitalizer* (Orlando: Renovate, 2015), 35.
3. Michael White and Tom Corcoran, *Rebuilt: Awakening the Faithful, Reaching the Lost, and Making Church Matter* (South Bend, IN: Ave Maria, 2013).

Chapter 1: Waiting for Things to Come Back Around

1. George Barna and David Kinnaman, *Churchless: Understanding Today's Unchurched and How to Connect with Them* (Carol Stream, IL: Tyndale, 2014), Locator 502–505 of 2574 (ebook).
2. Ibid., Locator 543 of 2574 (ebook).
3. Pew Research Center, 2014 U.S. Religious Landscape Study (Washington, D.C.: Pew Research Center, 2014).
4. Thom S. Rainer, *Autopsy of a Deceased Church: 12 Ways to Keep Yours Alive* (Nashville: B&H, 2014), 18.
5. Ibid., 100.
6. John Kotter, *Leading Change* (Cambridge: Harvard Business Review Press, 2012), 51–52.

7. Tacy M. Byham and Richard S. Wellins, *Your First Leadership Job: How Catalyst Leaders Bring Out the Best in Others* (Hoboken, NJ: John Wiley & Sons, 2015), 10–11.

8. Darrin Patrick and Mark DeVine, *Replant: How a Dying Church Can Grow Again* (Colorado Springs: David C Cook, 2014), Locator 45 of 1554 (ebook).

Chapter 2: Missing the Whale

1. James Mallon, *Divine Renovation* (Toronto: Novalis, 2014), 13.

2. Jim Collins and Jerry I. Porras, *Built to Last: Successful Habits of Visionary Companies* (New York: HarperCollins, 2011), xiv.

3. Bill Hybels, *Courageous Leadership* (Grand Rapids: Zondervan, 2002), 21.

4. Patrick Lencioni, *The Advantage: Why Organizational Health Trumps Everything Else in Business* (San Francisco: Jossey-Bass, 2012), 142–43.

Chapter 3: Barking Dogs

1. Judah Smith, *Jesus Is _____: Find a New Way to Be Human* (Nashville: Thomas Nelson, 2013), xvii.

2. Thom S. Rainer, and Eric Geiger, *Simple Church: Returning to God's Process for Making Disciples* (Nashville: B&H, 2006), 43.

3. Reggie Joiner, *Think Orange: Imagine the Impact When Church and Family Collide* (Colorado Springs: David C Cook, 2009), Locators 79 and 80 of 766 (ebook).

4. Andy Stanley, *Deep and Wide: Creating Churches Unchurched People Love to Attend* (Grand Rapids: Zondervan, 2012), 267.

Chapter 4: Silver Vega

1. Jim Collins, *Good to Great: Why Some Companies Make the Leap … and Others Don't* (New York: HarperCollins, 2011), 1.

2. Brad Lomenick, *The Catalyst Leader: 8 Essentials for Becoming a Change Maker* (Nashville: Thomas Nelson, 2013), 86–87.

3. Ed Stetzer and Mike Dodson, *Comeback Churches: How 300 Churches Turned Around and Yours Can, Too* (Nashville: Broadman & Holman, 2010), 83–84.

4. Timothy Keller, *Preaching: Communicating Faith in an Age of Skepticism* (New York: Viking, 2015), Locator 138–55 of 4183 (ebook).

5. Andy Stanley and Lane Jones, *Communicating for a Change: Seven Keys to Irresistible Communication* (Colorado Springs: Multnomah, 2006), 95.

Chapter 5: Don't Be Like Joshua

1. John Maxwell and Steven R. Covey, *The 21 Irrefutable Laws of Leadership: Follow Them and People Will Follow You* (Nashville: Thomas Nelson, 2007), 218–19, 224.

2. Brian Houston, *For This I Was Born: Aligning Your Vision to God's Cause* (Nashville: Thomas Nelson, 2008), Locator 583–96 of 1582 (ebook).

3. William Vanderbloemen and Warren Bird, *Next: Pastoral Succession That Works* (Grand Rapids: Baker, 2014), Locator 287, 305 of 4703 (ebook).

4. David Kinnaman, *You Lost Me: Why Young Christians Are Leaving Church* (Grand Rapids: Baker, 2011), Locator 53–54 of 437 (ebook).

Please visit

ForaNewGeneration.com

where you can download a Strategy Worksheet
for use in your church or organization